21st
Century
Lighting
Design

MW00356283

21st Century Lighting Design

Alyn Griffiths

BLOOMSBURY

Bloomsbury Visual Arts
An imprint of Bloomsbury Publishing Plc

50 Bedford Square   1385 Broadway
London   New York
WC1B 3DP   NY 10018
UK   USA

www.bloomsbury.com

Bloomsbury is a registered trade mark of Bloomsbury Publishing Plc

First published in Great Britain 2014

© Alyn Griffiths, 2014

Alyn Griffiths has asserted his right under the Copyright, Designs
and Patents Act, 1988, to be identified as author of this work.

All rights reserved. No part of this publication may be reproduced
or transmitted in any form or by any means, electronic or mechanical,
including photocopying, recording, or any information storage or retrieval
system, without prior permission in writing from the publishers.

No responsibility for loss caused to any individual or organization
acting on or refraining from action as a result of the material in this
publication can be accepted by Bloomsbury or the author.

British Library Cataloguing-in-Publication Data
A catalogue record for this book is available from the British Library.

ISBN: PB: 978-1-4725-0313-8

Library of Congress Cataloging-in-Publication Data
Griffiths, Alyn.
21st century lighting design/Alyn Griffiths
pages cm
ISBN 978-1-4725-0313-8 (pbk.)
1. Lighting, Architectural and decorative. I. Title. II. Title: Twenty-first century
lighting design.
NK2115.5.L5.G75 2014
729'.2809051—dc23
2013045866

Commissioning editor: **Simon Kean-Cowell**
Assistant editor: **Simon Longman**
Copy editor: **Ellen Grace**
Page and cover design: **Imagist**

Printed and bound in China

Acknowledgements

The author would like to thank all the designers, manufacturers and photographers who generously provided imagery for inclusion in this book. Thanks to Simon Keane-Cowell for proposing and commissioning *21st Century Lighting Design* and to Simon Longman for his help and guidance throughout the process. Special thanks to Ingo Maurer for providing his personal insight in the form of a fascinating foreword and to Kelly for her constant support and encouragement.

Image credits

Every effort has been made to identify and accurately credit the photographers and copyright holders of the images published in this book. Bloomsbury Publishing apologises for any unintentional inaccuracies in this information, which will be corrected in future editions of this work.

Publisher's notes

The projects in this book have been presented together with details of the company currently responsible for manufacturing the product. Where no manufacturer is credited, the designer or artist is responsible for producing the work. This applies particularly to some of the more conceptual designs, which may have been produced as one-off experiments or limited editions. To check availability or for more information it is recommended to contact the designer directly.

Garland by Tord Boontje is produced in the UK by Habitat (since 2002) and for international markets by Artecnica (since 2004).

Blossom by Tord Boontje and Lolita by Ron Arad are produced as part of the Swarovski Crystal Palace project: www.swarovskicrystalpalace.com

The Dream Cube Shanghai Corporate Pavilion project was a collaboration between ESI Design and architects Atelier FCJZ (China), with support from lighting specialists Full Flood (USA); media producer Spinifex (Australia); international technology firm PRG and exhibit fabricators Pico (China).

The dates supplied are completion dates and Bloomsbury Publishing has endeavoured to ensure that this information is correct at the time of publishing but apologises for any inaccuracies, which will be corrected in future editions of this work.

Contents

My New Flame (2012)
by Moritz Waldemeyer
for Ingo Maurer is a
contemporary reinvention
of the traditional candlestick
that uses LEDs to replicate
a flickering flame that will
never burn out.

A love affair with light
By Ingo Maurer

The twenty-first century has already produced some remarkable technical innovations, in the field of lighting, which I began to use with great enthusiasm at the earliest opportunity. Still, it saddens me that the iconic incandescent light bulb is being phased out and replaced with alternatives that lack its emotional appeal. The fire is missing from these new light sources: first we had fire, then we had lanterns and then the incandescent light bulb – now we need to develop these technologies so that people can really appreciate light again. It is important to realise that pushing boundaries – both technically and aesthetically – takes time and is not just about doing something for the sake of being new.

Inspiration for my projects comes from nature, from childhood memories and from my curiosity about materials, which I like to analyse and play with to try to determine suitable applications for them. At the beginning of my career I made the mistake of putting form ahead of light itself, but I quickly learned that form should not dictate the process – that the beauty of the light is always the most important thing. I try to make people more aware of the quality of light, which is directly connected to our emotions. Many people feel unhappy when they come home, and it is because their house is drearily lit – they don't realise they could improve their wellbeing by replacing this with a better quality of light. Light should be embracing and not too intrusive or overwhelming: it should create a wonderful spirit around you.

I never design a light because I think it will sell well; I am motivated by technical or aesthetic challenges and try to push boundaries wherever I can. There are companies who manufacture lighting products in huge numbers but this has never been a starting point for me. Some people think that what I do is art, not design, but I don't want to make art; I want to make something that I can enjoy and that might also bring joy to other people.

Over fifteen years ago my studio began experimenting with new light sources: we were the first to use LEDs for residential lighting products, and we worked on LED-based installations for private collectors. Through these projects we were interested in exploring all the possibilities this technology has to offer; it's very minimal, it doesn't take up much volume and you can dim it beautifully. We were also the first to work with OLED light sources, which are exciting because they don't require a reflector to direct the light. I remember visiting a conference in London and talking to producers of OLED technology who believed it was suddenly going to make them lots of money, but realistically, it needs to develop much more before it becomes commercially viable.

Today when I visit lighting fairs I see these new technologies everywhere, but they are often translated into products that make me shiver with cold because the designs miss what they are supposed to do. People need to recognise that technology is important and we're all curious about it, but the technology shouldn't be the focus of the design. The secret is to transform the technology into something...not romantic, but beautiful and pleasant to use, that expresses the joy of light.

Ingo Maurer is a German industrial designer who has been creating revolutionary lighting products since the 1960s. His experimental and emotive designs and pioneering work with new lighting technologies have contributed to his status as one of the world's most visionary designers.

Introduction

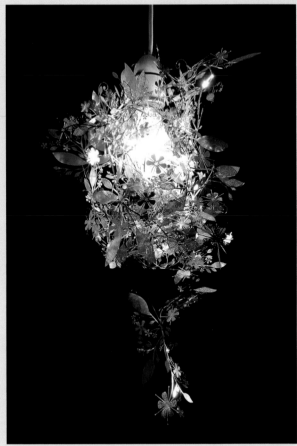

< Raimond
The Raimond lamp by
Belgian designer Raimond
Puts illustrates how
energy-efficient
alternatives to
incandescent light bulbs
are prompting a change
in the visual language of
lighting design.

∧ Garland
The intrinsic emotional
appeal of light continues
to encourage designers,
such as Tord Boontje, to
develop poetic and original
forms that challenge
existing typologies.

The twenty-first century has witnessed an unprecedented upheaval in the field of lighting design, with legislation banning the sale of the iconic incandescent light bulb forcing designers and manufacturers to re-evaluate every aspect of lighting. The sudden extinction of a light source that has been fundamental to the design of lighting products for over 130 years – along with the introduction of energy-efficient alternatives with distinctly different physical dimensions and luminescent properties – has rocked the industry and provoked an ongoing process of creative transformation that will ultimately shape our future relationship with light.

Many designers have embraced the technological revolution, excitedly exploring the functional potential of emerging light sources and the opportunity to develop new forms to fill the void left by redundant archetypes designed around the incandescent bulb. Others have adopted a more critical stance; saddened by the loss of a ubiquitous and much-loved object, they are dismissive of current replacements that lack the emotional appeal of their predecessor. The prevailing uncertainty about the most suitable direction for future lighting emphasises the vital role of design in ensuring that new technologies are applied intelligently and sympathetically to promote usability and enjoyment rather than simply celebrating novelty.

Although the introduction of alternatives to incandescent lighting represents the most dramatic catalyst for change within the industry, several other factors are affecting the evolution of contemporary lighting design. The postmodern sensibility that developed during the latter half of the twentieth century continues to inspire witty and introspective designs referencing past archetypes or challenging the forms and materials typically associated with lighting. Sophisticated computer modelling software and advanced manufacturing technologies enable the creation of incredibly complex and detailed designs, while digital control systems are transforming the way users interact with light. Simultaneously, there is a backlash against this digital revolution that has precipitated a resurgence in interest in craft and modern applications for natural or traditional materials, such as wood, glass and ceramic.

This book provides a survey of the most outstanding and original lighting products and installations created since the turn of the century (with one or two examples from the preceding year admitted due to their significant influence on the development of subsequent designs) and endeavours to explore the characteristics that make each light a pioneering or influential example of its type. Each project is identified by its title, the name of its designer or creator, the manufacturer (where relevant) and the year the piece was first produced. A selection of images representing the work are accompanied by brief captions and a description of its appearance, functionality and significance to the evolution of twenty-first century lighting design. The projects are separated into three categories – Form, Material and Technology – which represent the three key areas of innovation within lighting design. By comparing examples within these categories, it is possible to identify strikingly different approaches to the design and manufacture of contemporary lighting. Inevitably, there is some crossover between the categories, as many lighting projects aim to balance all three aspects; however the decision as to where each design should sit has been made based on its most fundamental or extreme characteristic.

As the emphasis of this book is on innovation, the selected projects are predominantly from the field of domestic lighting, rather than from the commercial field, whose solutions are used to provide ambient lighting in offices, institutions and industrial environments. Although the introduction of alternative light sources will gradually alter lighting design within these areas, there are currently few examples that represent a radical departure from the solutions that have existed for several decades. In the Technology section, however, there is a notable lack of domestic products due to the prohibitively expensive processes currently required to manufacture the latest alternative light sources. These technologies remain the preserve of artists and designers who operate outside of the typical constraints imposed by mass production methods. Often the aim of such technological experimentation is to explore potential applications for new light sources through groundbreaking objects and installations that regularly cross over into the fields of architecture, fashion, performance art and sculpture.

The introduction of advanced lighting technologies into the domestic environment looks set to be a gradual process. The benefits of the various emerging light sources need to be explained to consumers who are accustomed to incandescent light bulbs, and prices need to drop before these new products will be widely accepted. In the meantime, consumers are settling for replacing their burned out incandescent bulbs with like-for-like energy-saving alternatives. While this transition takes place, designers continue to explore new techniques and approaches within the parameters established by traditional lighting typologies. The familiar properties of pendant lamps, floor lamps, wall lamps, table lamps, task lights and chandeliers still provide the foundations for many experimental interpretations of form, material, scale and interaction.

Despite the legislative and technological turmoil affecting the lighting industry, and the radical responses this has provoked, the purpose of artificial lighting remains the same as ever – to enhance the comfort, functionality and attractiveness of its environment. Lighting products need to provide ambient, directional or task lighting that helps to define space and enables us to work, socialise and move around after dark and indoors. They should direct or diffuse light as appropriate to avoid glare, while promoting the emotional associations with safety and warmth that make light integral to our everyday lives. Whatever the light source and however a product is designed, these key functions must be fulfilled for it to be deemed successful. From futuristic forms that express the progressive properties of new light sources, to intelligent applications of classic materials that create comfortingly familiar effects, twenty-first century lighting design provides plenty of examples of projects that demonstrate a contemporary commitment to innovation and imagination.

Alternative light sources

Not since Thomas Edison patented the first commercially viable version of the incandescent light bulb in 1879 has the lighting industry experienced such an epochal event as the recent introduction and implementation of legislation governing the efficiency and performance of light sources. The need to reduce energy consumption and minimise mankind's impact on the planet's finite natural resources began to infiltrate the public consciousness towards the end of the twentieth century, as consumers were encouraged to consider the importance of issues including recycling, cradle-to-cradle manufacturing and the provenance and ethical credentials of materials. A European Union directive banning the sale of incandescent bulbs became fully operational in September 2012 and similar initiatives are gradually being enforced by regional governments around the world, prompting an immediate need for energy-efficient replacements.

The first and most straightforward alternative to emerge was the compact fluorescent lamp (CFL), whose twisted gas-filled tubes are already a familiar sight in many households due to their ability to fit existing fixtures and emulate many of the properties of incandescent light bulbs. Although the initial cost of a CFL is higher than that of an equivalent incandescent bulb, their longevity and low energy consumption saves money over time, an important factor when trying to attract consumers who are skeptical about the need for change. Light-emitting diodes (LEDs) have also evolved from their initial use solely in digital displays and electronic equipment to become a viable option for ambient or task lighting. Declining production costs are assisting the availability of LEDs, while their functional versatility and minimal dimensions appeal to designers looking to explore new directions for lighting. The development of light-emitting materials made from organic or inorganic compounds that release energy as light when an electrical current is applied represents a radical departure from the aesthetic and functional properties of traditional light bulbs. These materials are being translated into paper-thin light sources such as organic light-emitting diodes (OLEDs) and glowing fibres that have already been trialled in several prototypal products and installations.

Each of the alternatives to incandescent lighting has advantages and issues associated with it, which are explained more comprehensively in the introduction to the Technology section. Pioneering projects that explore the physical properties of LEDs, OLEDs and other electroluminescent materials offer a glimpse of a possible future. Although it will inevitably take time for emerging technologies to become affordable and refined enough to be widely accepted as replacements for familiar light sources, the transition has begun and there is no going back.

< Plumen 001
Plumen 001 by lighting brand Hulger and designer Samuel Wilkinson offers a more attractive alternative to standard energy-saving light bulbs.

∨ Sonumbra
Light-emitting materials, such as the electroluminescent fibres used in Loop.pH's Sonumbra installation, have significantly different physical properties to conventional light sources.

^ **Fall of the Damned**
Advances in computer
software and digital
manufacturing enable
lighting designers to realise
incredibly complex shapes
like the Fall of the Damned
chandelier by Luc Merx.

A digital revolution

Alongside the introduction of alternative lighting
technologies, the twenty-first century has also
witnessed incredible advances in computer software
and manufacturing processes, which have affected all
aspects of the design industry, including architecture,
graphics, furniture and lighting. Computer-aided design
(CAD) software enables designers to create impossibly
complex forms that can be manipulated and rendered
to simulate a product's appearance without the need
to build a physical representation. Sophisticated
engineering programmes also facilitate the analysis
of an object's structural integrity and help to determine
the most suitable and efficient production method.
The blobby, undulating or intersecting forms
popularised by architects such as Zaha Hadid, Daniel
Liebeskind and Frank Gehry around the turn of the
century represent the most visible manifestation of
these principles, but their influence extends to all
three-dimensional design disciplines and is particularly
evident in the flowing forms of Ross Lovegrove's lighting
designs for Artemide (see pages 030, 031, 230, and 231)
and Yamagiwa (see page 027, 040 and 041).

The recent surge of complex and elaborate forms in
product design can also be attributed to the evolution
of computer-controlled machinery that can cut, mill or
etch finely detailed objects from solid materials, and
additive manufacturing technologies that translate
data into three-dimensional forms by printing them
in successive layers. The virtually unlimited aesthetic
possibilities facilitated by these revolutionary processes
have informed the design of many contemporary lighting
products. With the freedom to visualise and realise
almost any shape, the ongoing challenge for lighting
designers is to identify appropriate uses for these
techniques that result in a necessary synergy between
light, form, material and process.

The operation of lighting products is another area
that has undergone significant change in recent years,
due to the introduction of sensors and remote or
intuitive methods of controlling light sources. The act of
pushing, pulling or twisting a switch or dimmer to adjust
a light suddenly seems old-fashioned now that devices
such as smartphones and tablets enable the brightness
and colour of light to be controlled remotely. Motion
sensors that can turn lights on when someone enters
a room and infrared switches used in products such as
Ron Arad's PizzaKobra lamp (pages 042 and 043) and
the Kelvin LED task light by Antonio Citterio and Toan
Nguyen (see pages 176 and 177) indicate that interaction
with lighting is becoming increasingly less tangible.

Sensor-based systems linked to lighting are proving
particularly influential among a new generation of
designers keen to exploit their interactive potential.
These digital pioneers are educated in the skills required

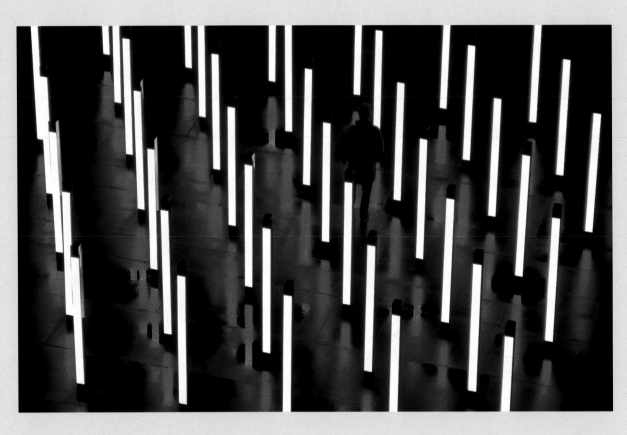

❮ **Volume**
UVA's Volume installation combines contemporary lighting with motion sensors to create an immersive interactive environment.

to programme computer software and hack electronic devices so they perform specific tasks when prompted by a variety of stimuli. Contemporary light sources can be adapted so their behaviour responds to anything, from sound and movement to information gathered from the Internet. Examples of this fusion between lighting and digital media exists on varying scales, ranging from permanent installations covering the entire façade of a building, to temporary site-specific artworks designed to engage the public. Light acts as the medium these digital design projects use to draw attention to the changing nature of the relationships between people and objects in contemporary society.

A new look for lighting

Developments in every field of design are influenced by a variety of external factors, including the prevalent economic conditions and societal mood – both of which have a profound effect on the objectives of designers and manufacturers. The new millennium was viewed by many as a fresh start; a chance to vanquish the past and adopt a progressive approach that would spur mankind on to new heights of creative sophistication and technical achievement. Its dawn coincided with a period of economic prosperity across most of the developed world that resulted in a revival of interest in creating highly personal interiors – defined by expressive and playful products.

Within the lighting industry, the emergence of alternative light sources and advances in digital design and manufacturing processes have further emphasised the need for change, encouraging and supporting an anarchic attitude among designers who recognise that established rules dictating the appropriate use of form and materials are becoming outdated and ripe for reinterpretation. The dramatic downturn that struck in 2008 stunted the global economy and provoked a re-evaluation of necessity versus superfluity that affected all aspects of design; however, our dependence on light continues to attract designers to explore its aesthetic potential, and the lighting industry's dedication to positioning itself at the forefront of sustainable innovation has helped it to continue evolving throughout this difficult period for design.

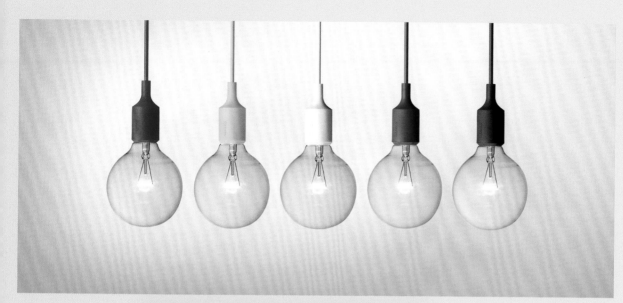

‹ E27
Mattias Ståhlbom's design
for an elegant socket and
electrical cord epitomises
a contemporary desire to
re-examine every aspect
of lighting products.

L Bourgie
Ferruccio Laviani's Bourgie
table lamp evinces a
popular twenty-first
century trend for combining
historical visual references
with contemporary materials.

During the early part of the twentieth century, design was dominated by the doctrines of Modernism, and a philosophy of designing for need was prompted by the two destructive World Wars. Gradually, during the second half of the century, reactionary movements intent on reintroducing decoration, pattern and humour to design began to emerge and gain momentum. Italy played a crucial role in this creative upsurge, with the Italian government supporting collaborations between design and industry as part of its plans to reinvigorate the country's economy following World War II. The 'readymade' products and lighting solutions created by influential designers, including the Castiglioni brothers in the 1960s, and the sculptural designs of radical groups such as Studio Alchimia and Memphis in the 1970s and 1980s, inspired successive generations of designers to challenge familiar forms and product typologies. Italy's established manufacturing and craft expertise, particularly in glass making, underpinned its influence on the evolution of lighting design. Despite the onset of globalisation and the redistribution of manufacturing to regions such as Asia and the Indian subcontinent, Italy remains a powerful force in lighting design and Italian firms are responsible for almost a quarter of the projects included in this book. The Italian flair for creativity and ingenuity is a perfect match for the expressive quality of light.

Amid all the stylistic posturing and conceptual experimentation that has occurred within lighting design since the turn of the century, there are several designers who remain focused on rational and sensitive solutions that quietly promote light's intrinsic utility and beauty. Barber Osgerby's Tab light (see pages 072 and 073) and the Piani table lamp by the French brothers, Ronan and Erwan Bouroullec (see pages 074 and 075), represent entirely original forms that manage to be both elegant and intuitive, while Swedish designer Mattias Ståhlbom's E27 rubber socket and cord (see page 078 and 079) focuses on refining the part of a light that is normally hidden so that it becomes attractive in its own right. These lights may not be the most aesthetically, technically or intellectually challenging products of this century, but they are among the most popular, and their timeless appeal and attention to detail will enable them to outlive more flamboyant contemporaries. The look of twenty-first century lighting has played an important role in shaping the current creative landscape and will continue to do so, as lighting remains one of the most visible and attractive disciplines for the world's top designers.

The changing role of materials

When designing any lighting product, a key decision is how to diffuse the light, a decision that requires an expert knowledge of materials and their properties. Traditionally, the glare created by the contrast of a bright light source against its surroundings is combated by adding a diffuser to filter the light, or a reflector to conceal it completely and project it onto nearby surfaces. Fabric, paper and glass are the materials most commonly used as diffusers, as their varying degrees of translucency allow the amount of light passing through to be controlled. The different ways in which materials diffuse or reflect light are a constant source of inspiration for designers. The twenty-first century has seen continuing experimentation in this area, from Marc Sadler's specially developed composites (see pages 148 and 149), to the printed circuit boards used by Matali Crasset to both supply power to and diffuse light from LED bulbs (see pages 160 and 161). Almost any material can be used to reduce glare, so the test for twenty-first century designers is to identify original and intelligent applications for either classic or cutting-edge materials.

The changing landscape of lighting design since the turn of the century – and particularly the introduction of new light sources that initially failed to replicate the warm light provided by incandescent bulbs – has provoked a revival in the number of designers engaging with craft processes and tactile, natural materials. This echoes a wider trend within product design, which has seen designers adopting handcrafted techniques and raw finishes in reaction to dematerialisation resulting from the rapid rise of digital technologies. Lighting designers are turning to mouth-blown glass, untreated wood and ceramics, as well as warm metals, such as copper and brass. These materials come to life when used in conjunction with light and express their character through the grain, patina or tone of their surfaces. The 28 series pendant lamp, designed by Vancouver-based Omer Arbel (see pages 090, 114 and 115), celebrates the uniqueness of mouth-blown glass, while Tom Dixon's lampshades made from copper, brass and bronze accentuate the familiar glow and crisp reflections these metals produce (see pages 122, 123, 126, 127, 156 and 157). The relationship between light and natural or handcrafted materials has a timeless appeal that designers continue to revisit and that offers a counterpoint to the relentless technological progress affecting the industry.

In the future, the need for materials that control the performance of light may be negated by the evolution of advanced light sources such as OLEDs and electroluminescent materials, which emit light across a flat surface and don't require additional diffusion. LEDs are already being used in many task lights because they can provide a direct light without the need for a reflector to focus the beam. Although cutting-edge technologies make the use of traditional diffusers and reflectors appear outdated, their applications are largely limited to function-led products. Most domestic lighting scenarios rely on materials that can provide the intrinsic sense of warmth and tactility that is such a valuable part of light's appeal. The texture, colour and patina of materials add to a product's character, something that technology is unable to replicate.

⌐ Ruminant Bloom
Lighting offers an opportunity for extreme material experimentation, like Julia Lohmann's lamps made from preserved animal stomachs.

⌄ Lighthouse
Traditional materials, such as glass, still inspire designers to develop original lighting products like the Bouroullec brothers' Lighthouse lamp.

< **Dream Cube**
The interactive potential
of future lighting is
demonstrated by projects
such as ESI Design's
Dream Cube Shanghai
Corporate Pavilion.

A bright future

The surge of technological developments affecting the design and manufacture of lighting products makes it difficult to predict how the landscape of lighting design will evolve as the twenty-first century progresses. It seems inevitable that the immediate future will involve a gradual acceptance of like-for-like replacements for the incandescent light bulb, which replicate its dimensions and performance using CFL and LED light sources. In the medium term, the availability of brighter and more affordable LEDs with improved colour temperatures will present an opportunity to reconsider the size and shape of lighting fixtures, while more sophisticated systems incorporated into the structure of new homes will allow for greater control and customisation of ambient lighting.

Eventually, the evolution of electroluminescent materials and paper-thin light-emitting surfaces will enable lighting products to disappear completely into walls, ceilings or furniture. Invisible inbuilt light sources linked to sensors will respond to our needs and behaviours, providing suitable illumination when prompted by minimal gestures or even more intuitive forms of interaction. Motion sensors will be able to track our movement and provide light wherever we go; surfaces will suddenly start to glow when we touch them or place something on them; and the brightness and colour of light will adjust itself depending on the time of day or the activity taking place around it. All of these things are already achievable, but must undergo significant refinement before they become widely available.

It is particularly difficult to predict how long it will take for consumers to accept and adopt new technologies. The basic requirement of lighting – to compensate for a lack of natural daylight – has been successfully fulfilled for centuries by products as simple as the candlestick. The revolutionary potential of alternative light sources must be tempered by considering where these technologies can add value and make the experience of light more pleasurable and intuitive. Twenty-first century lighting has engaged with progressive technologies, but familiar forms and materials that have been associated with light for generations continue to influence the design of new products. Although the light sources themselves are changing, the role of lighting design remains the same – to balance form, material and technology and create products that satisfy practical needs in appropriate, attractive, and sometimes, spectacular ways.

Form

L   Skygarden
Skygarden, by Marcel
Wanders, exhibits a
postmodern sensibility,
combining a contemporary
form with historical
decoration.

Light has the intrinsic ability to attract attention and instinctively invoke feelings of safety and comfort. These properties have always appealed to designers seeking an expressive and familiar outlet for their personal methodologies. The creative freedom that lighting offers is another key reason for its popularity. So long as a light can support itself or be safely suspended, and the electronics and light source are protected, there are few functional restrictions that dictate how it must look. Consequently, each era of design features defining examples of lighting products that encapsulate the spirit and aesthetic approach of the time. From Louis Comfort Tiffany's stained glass masterpieces of the late-nineteenth century, to contemporary products incorporating the latest technologies, lighting design acts as a reliable gauge for the evolution of formal and technical innovation in industrial design.

The aesthetics of twenty-first century lighting can be attributed to several key social and technological factors, particularly the globalisation of design and culture, the development of computer-aided design and manufacturing processes, and the introduction of efficient alternative light sources. The result is a rapidly evolving aesthetic landscape that revokes characterisation and embraces references from the past, present and future.

The look of early twentieth century design was dominated by the ascension of Modernism, which rejected ornament in favour of efficiency and rationalism. In the second half of the century, Modernism's 'less is more' doctrine came under attack from proponents of more decorative and characterful styles. Following the devastation and hardship inflicted by the two World Wars, design was called upon to respond to the desire for more lively, irreverent and instantly gratifying products. Stylistic preferences fluctuated over the ensuing decades in accordance with the prevailing economic and social conditions, but as the twenty-first century approached, the postmodern predilection for vibrant, witty and self-referential products continued to influence design.

Excitement and expectations aroused by the arrival of the twenty-first century helped generate a mood of optimism across the developed world – supported by a buoyant economy and dramatic revolutions in computing and communication technologies. The Internet facilitated the dissemination of information on an unprecedented scale, improving global connectivity and the exchange of ideas. Affordable international travel offered designers access to a superfluity of visual and cultural stimuli and enabled transcontinental collaborations between designers and manufacturers. Meanwhile, the development of computer-aided design tools and manufacturing processes suddenly enabled designers to visualise forms and quickly realise prototypes that were previously unthinkable. These factors contributed to an 'anything goes' attitude within industrial design. Global and local references, historical and futuristic iconography, and cutting-edge technologies all combined to create an incoherent and unpredictable aesthetic landscape. Lighting design, in particular,

encouraged designers to eschew established typologies and functional expectations in favour of sculptural statements that put form at the forefront of the creative process.

The anarchic aesthetic approach of many contemporary lighting designers can be traced back to the pioneering postmodern architecture and design collectives of the 1970s and 1980s, including Studio Alchimia and Memphis. Their experimental, decorative furniture and products were predominantly designed as provocative exhibition pieces, and therefore tended to emphasise sculptural forms over functionality. In reaction to the perceived sterile and dogmatic tendencies of Modernism, they employed riotous colour and pattern, as well as references to previous artistic and architectural styles. Several examples of products in this section demonstrate a similar evocative and iconoclastic approach, typically using archetypal or familiar historical forms as a starting point for ironic and playful new products. The familiar motifs of the candlestick, the chandelier and the traditional table or floor standing lamp are regularly reinterpreted in surprising ways to highlight a deliberate anomaly or stylistic intervention. The Bourgie table lamp, by Italian designer Ferruccio Laviani, is a good example of this. The outline of the three identical polycarbonate pieces that form its tripod base resembles a simplified version of a scrolling Baroque form. By contrasting this ornate classical shape with an inexpensive everyday material, the product elicits design's ability to add value through decoration. Charles Trevelyan's Titanic Lamp transforms the traditional turned-wood table lamp into a witty reference to the ill-fated ship by slicing the base and shade at an angle so the lamp appears to be sinking. We recognise the appearance and purpose of these objects, but their status as lighting products is merely a vehicle for an idea or a visual gag.

Contemporary references also find their way into lighting projects in the shape of 'ready-made' designs, such as Ron Gilad's chandelier, consisting of sixteen articulated task lamps arranged around a central frame, which alludes to the standardisation of mass-produced design. Philippe Starck's provocative Gun Lamps are an unambiguous symbol of violence and the commodity-driven culture that drives it. These designers aren't afraid to use found objects and contemporary iconography to create humorous sculptural products, with illumination supplementing the theatrical aesthetic.

As well as looking to the past and the present, the dawn of a new millennium inevitably prompted designers to conjure a vision of the future. Contemporary lighting designs offer different interpretations of future aesthetics, from slick retro-futuristic forms, to complex shapes that imply an organic intelligence. Some products employ streamlined, space-age forms, such as the gleaming pebble-shaped Loop lamp by VW+BS, or Sebastian Wrong's fluid, glossy Spun light. The Pipe light, by Herzog & de Meuron, extends from the ceiling or wall like a robotic tentacle and can be bent and twisted to direct the light. The progressive appearance of these products is supported, and in some cases enabled, by the advanced techniques used to create them. In particular, the refinement of parametric computer software has revolutionised the processes used to generate form. These programmes enable three-dimensional shapes to be created by adjusting a set of initial parameters, which in turn affects the entire form. British designer Ross Lovegrove has pioneered the application of parametric software in product design with his organically influenced creations. His designs often exploit the software's ability to efficiently distribute material according to where it is structurally necessary. The Mercury collection for Italian brand Artemide consists of clusters of pebble-shaped elements suspended from the ceiling, while the complex organic structure of the Andromeda luminaire for Japanese firm Yamagiwa would have been extremely difficult to realise without sophisticated computerised techniques.

Besides the advances taking place in computer software, new manufacturing technologies also have a profound affect on the design of contemporary lighting. Digitally controlled processes, such as laser cutting, photo etching and CNC milling, can produce objects of staggering complexity, based on three-dimensional computer models. The manufacturing method with perhaps the most disruptive potential is additive layer manufacturing – the process of building a physical object from successive layers of printed material. Originally called rapid prototyping, the technique was developed by the engineering industry to produce models or prototype parts. Although additive layering processes still take a relatively long time to produce objects in comparison with conventional moulding and machining techniques, the technology has already produced several experimental projects that demonstrate its groundbreaking capabilities.

Belgian company Materialise has pioneered the development of additive layer manufacturing through its creative division .MGX, which regularly commissions designers to create experimental products that help to promote the benefits of the process. An early collaboration with Finnish designer Janne Kyttanen resulted in the LILY.MGX series (2004), comprising floor and table lamps with a delicate form resembling layers of petals surrounding the light source. Other designers have stretched the capabilities of the process further by developing products with precise, mathematically inspired textural surfaces, interlocking shapes or forms within forms. Integrating light enhances the astonishing detail and unusual textures that can be achieved using this production method. Additive manufacturing has the potential to radically alter the ways in which products are designed, manufactured and consumed, allowing any object to be reproduced anywhere in the world easily and cheaply. The development of products and systems that exploit this potential and support customisation of the final form will be a recurring theme in lighting design in forthcoming years.

Digital software and manufacturing technologies are redefining the tools designers use to create and produce lighting products, but the enforced extinction of the incandescent light bulb and its replacement with energy-efficient alternatives also plays a significant role in informing the shape of contemporary lighting.

New light sources, such as light-emitting diodes (LEDs), bear little resemblance to conventional bulbs; therefore designers are tasked with identifying a suitable aesthetic language that befits their physical characteristics and progressive qualities. Examples of particularly innovative uses for these new light sources can be found in the Technology section of this book, but their gradual introduction in recent years has already resulted in some visually groundbreaking products. The Leaf lamp by Yves Béhar, for example, confronts the alien nature of LED technology by sheathing the light source in an organic form that manages to be both futuristic and familiar. Its extremely thin profile deliberately enhances the defining physical difference between efficient LED technology and the more bulky traditional light bulb. The product's sleek minimalism encapsulates an important new direction for the form of lighting products, which aims to celebrate the advantages of new energy-efficient and space-efficient technologies.

The introduction of alternative light sources further complicates the already incoherent look of twenty-first century lighting. The unfamiliar aesthetic, as well as new functional and luminous properties of these lighting technologies, offers a blank canvas for designers to exploit in highly personal ways. The ongoing evolution of digital design and manufacturing tools and the lack of a dominant ideology guiding stylistic development across all design disciplines also contribute to the unprecedented creative freedom afforded to contemporary designers. In this time of aesthetic abundance, aesthetic trends continue to emerge, expand and dissipate with frantic regularity. This liberal attitude and the relentless technological revolution will sustain a culture of creativity and diversity within industrial design, and lighting products will continue to act as an important indicator of progress and key aesthetic developments.

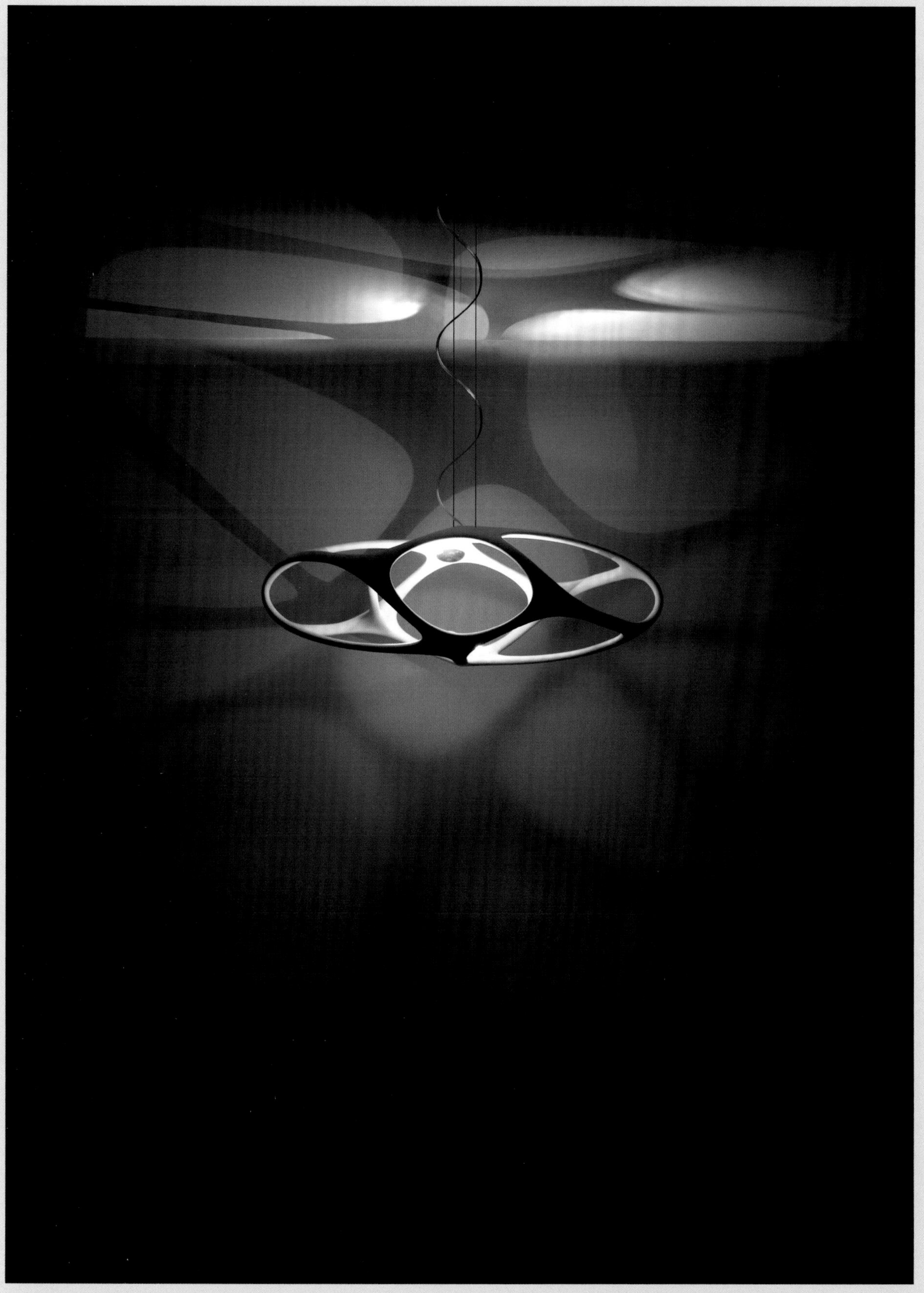

< Andromeda
The futuristic form of Ross Lovegrove's pendant shade is designed using sophisticated parametric computer software.

⌐ The organic shape of this standing lamp was developed using cutting-edge parametric software.

∧ A halogen up-lighter provides ambient lighting, and an adjustable LED spotlight is hidden behind a semi-transparent cover.

The fluid form of this lamp is typical of the amorphous aesthetic regularly employed by Iraqi-British architect Zaha Hadid and her London studio. It was developed using advanced parametric design software, which has played a crucial part in the creation of the studio's many iconic buildings, including the MAXXI Museum in Rome and the Aquatics Centre for the London 2012 Olympic Games.

Drawing inspiration from nature and the structure of trees, the lamp's base morphs into a stand, which then splits into branches supporting a cantilevered section that houses the light sources. A downward-pointing LED spotlight and an indirect halogen up-lighter offer different lighting options. The light output can be controlled using touch-sensitive power and dimmer switches located on the lamp's body. The organic form resembles the intricate biomorphic designs of early twentieth century architects, such as Antoni Gaudí and Hector Guimard, which were painstakingly produced in wood, stone and iron. Genesy, however, is made using a fast, precise and infinitely repeatable injection-moulding process.

Product	Designer	Manufacturer	Date
Mercury	**Ross Lovegrove**	**Artemide**	**2007**

‹ Mercury is typical of Ross Lovegrove's desire to invoke the dynamic forms created by nature.

A reflector bounces light onto the metallic surfaces of the pebble-shaped units.

The sculptural form of the Mercury collection epitomises Ross Lovegrove's fascination with forms created by natural phenomena. Designed for Italian brand Artemide, the product exemplifies the use of flowing plastic forms in architecture and design that were a feature of the new millennium's fledgling years. Each of the injection-moulded thermoplastic units resembles a pebble that has been polished smooth by the sea and is treated with a metallic coating that reflects its surroundings. LEDs concealed in the upper surfaces of some of the units project light onto a stainless steel reflector, which disperses it across the fluid surfaces.

Born in Cardiff, Wales in 1958, Lovegrove studied industrial design at Manchester Polytechnic before completing a master's at the Royal College of Art in London in 1983. He worked at Frog Design in Germany on products including Apple computers and the Sony Walkman before moving to Paris to take on a role as a consultant with furniture manufacturer Knoll. Since returning to London in 1986, Lovegrove has established himself at the vanguard of the parametric design movement with a succession of products influenced by scientific principles.

Product
Pipe

Designer
Herzog & de Meuron

Manufacturer
Artemide

Date
2002

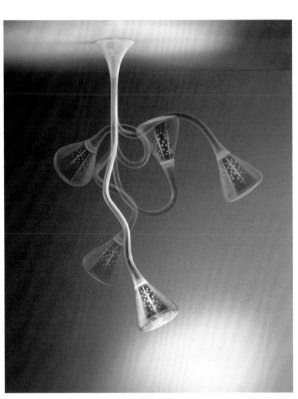

‹ Perforations in the aluminium reflector create a speckled pattern of light on the external surface of the light source.

L A flexible steel tube enables the Pipe light to be manipulated into position.

The tentacle-like form of Herzog & de Meuron's Pipe light can be bent and twisted by the user, allowing light to be directed as desired. The flexible steel tube is sheathed in natural platinic silicone and terminates in a polygonal cone-shaped diffuser. Light is focused by an aluminium reflector dotted with variously sized perforations that allow a mottled pattern of light spots to emanate from its surface.

Swiss architects Jacques Herzog and Pierre de Meuron originally designed the Pipe light for the offices of the Helvetia insurance company in

St Gallen, Switzerland (1998-2002) before applying the same principle to the design of fittings, including wall-mounted televisions used in the 2000-2003 development of the Prada Epicenter in Aoyama, Tokyo. Herzog and de Meuron head one of the world's most acclaimed and innovative architectural practices, known for its experimental approach and aptitude for redefining building typologies. This anarchic attitude is evident in the design of Pipe, which eschews traditional preconceptions of a pendant light in favour of futuristic form and functional innovation.

British designer Sebastian Wrong studied sculpture in Norwich and London before founding his own design and manufacturing company in 1996. In 2002 he was invited to present his Spun Light at the Milan Furniture Fair, where it attracted the attention of one of Italy's leading lighting brands, Flos, who subsequently put it into production. Spun Light's sleek aesthetic quickly helped establish it as a modern classic, earning Wrong a prestigious Red Dot Design Award and provoking a slew of imitations. The elegant silhouette and glossy finish are inspired by fluid dynamics, and the spun metal form is produced using precise contemporary fabrication techniques.

Wrong's appreciation for the skills and processes required to create cutting-edge products was instrumental in the launch of British design brand Established & Sons, which he co-founded in 2005. There, he oversaw the development of a portfolio of products, united by their formal and technical ingenuity, and created several notable designs of his own, including the Font Clock and Wrong Woods furniture, in collaboration with the artist Richard Woods.

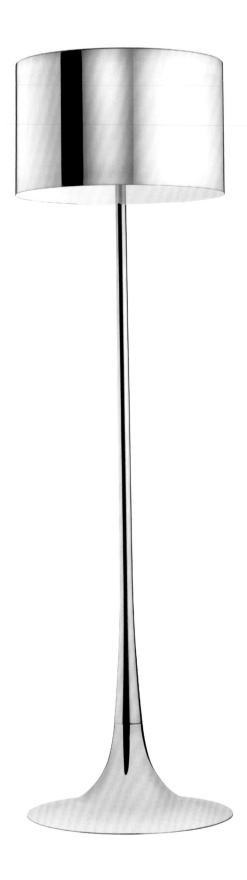

∟ The slick form of the
Spun Light is inspired by
fluid dynamics.

❯ The tapering
spun metal frame and
diffuser rely on precise
manufacturing methods.

Product	Designer	Manufacturer	Date
Loop	**VW+BS**	**Fontana Arte**	**2003**

⌐ Loop consists of two identical chromed steel parts hinged around an offset spindle.

∧ The light output can be adjusted by rotating the upper section to reveal an illuminated surface.

Loop conceals a light source between two matching stainless steel parts connected by an offset spindle that allows the top section to swivel over the edge of the lower part. The amount of light dispersed can be increased simply by revealing more of the illuminated surface between the sections. The flattened spherical form has a diameter of 50cm, which gives it a sculptural presence on the floor or tabletop, and its smooth, pebble-like appearance is enhanced by a highly reflective chrome finish.

First exhibited as part of a collection of lighting products at the 2001 Designersblock exhibition in London, Loop helped to launch its designers into the international spotlight. Singaporean Voon Wong and Malaysian Benson Saw are based in London and their multidisciplinary consultancy VW+BS has offices in Singapore and Kuala Lumpur. Wong studied architecture in Singapore and London before working for architects, including Zaha Hadid, while Saw graduated in mechanical engineering at Boston University in 1999. A combination of spatial awareness and technical innovation defines their work, which spans architecture, interior and industrial design.

Product
O-Space

Designer
**Luca Nichetto and
Gianpietro Gai**

Manufacturer
Foscarini

Date
2003

‹ The futuristic form
of the O-Space pendant
resembles a spaceship
hovering in mid-air.

This sculptural pendant shade is the result of a collaboration between Italian designers Luca Nichetto and Gianpietro Gai. It takes the unusual form of a compressed sphere with two oval sections spliced from its surface. The product's streamlined, futuristic aesthetic is heightened when a halogen light source hidden in the bottom section is turned on, producing an ethereal glow that fills the internal void. Glass diffusers in the top and bottom surfaces project a direct light upwards and downwards, while the shell's smooth interior helps create an even glow that emanates from the large apertures.

Nichetto and Gai worked closely with the materials research and product development team at lighting specialist Foscarini (for whom Nichetto was a consultant from 2001–2003) and chose to produce O-Space from expanded polyurethane, a lightweight and durable plastic more commonly associated with the manufacture of electronic components and mouldings for domestic appliances. The material's smooth, matt surface helps to accentuate the curvaceous form and the contrasting edge marking the transition between the internal and external surfaces.

⌐ Direct light is projected up and down and a diffused light escapes from the holes on either side.

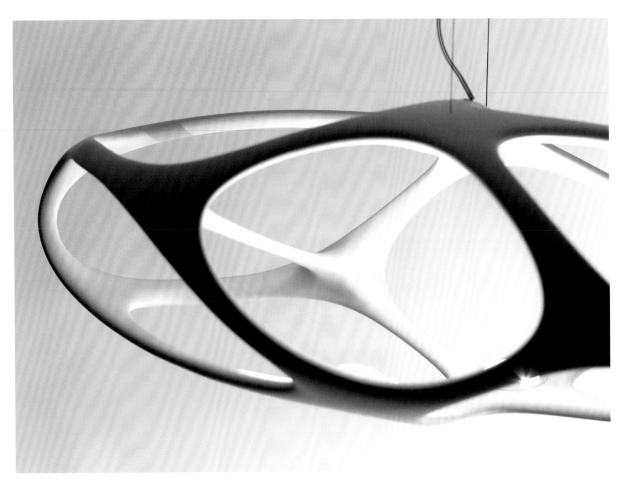

‹ Clusters of LEDs are embedded in the surfaces where the branches intersect.

⌐ Andromeda's organic form was created using optimisation software that distributes material where it is structurally required.

The light yet robust skeletal structure of this pendant light is typical of Ross Lovegrove's fascination with organic form and with replicating nature's efficient and elegant designs using contemporary manufacturing methods. In its shape and construction, Andromeda is closely related to several of Lovegrove's earlier projects, including the iconic Go Chair launched by Bernhardt in 2001. The lamp's fluid form is created using computer software that optimises the distribution of material to provide support only where it is needed.

Clusters of LEDs embedded at the intersections of the polyurethane structure project light onto magnetised mirror reflectors that can be moved and adjusted to alter the angle and distribution of the light. This creates a dramatic contrast between the brightly illuminated central branches and the shadows that define the exterior. As well as providing an eye-catching sculptural statement within the room, Andromeda casts a web of overlapping and intertwining shadows onto nearby surfaces.

Product	Designer	Manufacturer	Date
PizzaKobra	**Ron Arad**	**iGuzzini**	**2007**

❮ The PizzaKobra light folds flat when not in use and unfurls to provide directional task lighting.

∧ An LED on the end of the coil indicates the location of the touch-sensitive power switch.

The chromed-steel spiral that forms Ron Arad's PizzaKobra light is divided into sections joined by sophisticated hinges that enable it to unfurl in myriad ways. In its flat, dormant state, the disc-like form is less than 2cm high but can stretch to over 70cm when fully extended. Six LEDs on the underside of the final loop provide a bright task light that can be directed by manoeuvring the articulated sections. A standby light on the tip of the spiral signals the position of the touch-sensitive on-off switch.

Following his graduation from London's Architectural Association in 1979, Israeli-born Arad founded his own design and manufacturing company, One Off, in 1981 and quickly attracted attention with his designs for robust ready-made products and welded steel furniture. Arad's consistent experimentation with materials and technologies has resulted in a steady flow of groundbreaking projects for many of the world's leading manufacturers.

Product	Designer	Manufacturer	Date
Leaf	**Yves Béhar**	**Herman Miller**	**2006**

‹ Leaf is formed from two twisted aluminium sections that are hinged to enable the light to be directed as required.

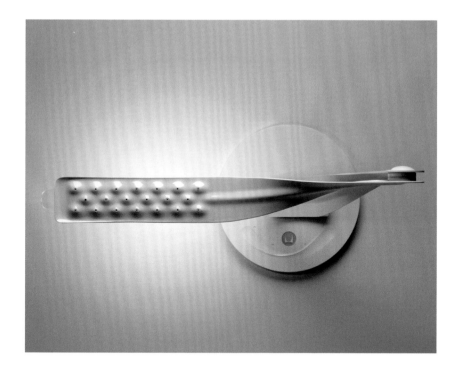

Leaf translates the functional versatility of LEDs into a tactile experience by encouraging the user to adjust the intensity and warmth of the light using a touch-sensitive groove in the lamp's base. The lamp's organic form also serves as a counterpoint to the cutting-edge technology. A slimline aluminium profile houses 20 LEDs in an upper section that can be directed for task lighting or folded down to create more ambient light. The heat generated by this many LEDs would normally make the surfaces too hot to touch, but proprietary heat distribution means the metal remains cool without the need for an auxiliary fan. This helps reduce energy consumption and bolsters the lamp's ecological credentials.

It took four years to design and engineer the product, which is the first to offer a choice between warm mood lighting and cool light for working. This innovation, combined with the lamp's organic shape, exemplifies Béhar's desire to humanise technology – in this case by improving the experience of interacting with LED lighting.

⌐ Dimples in the upper surface indicate the position of the bulbs.

Product
FL/Y

Designer
Ferruccio Laviani

Manufacturer
Kartell

Date
2003

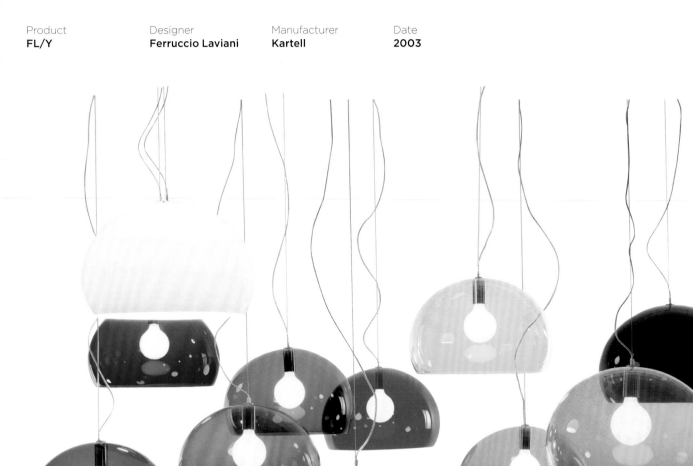

‹   The transparent
plastic shade of the FL/Y
pendant is available in a
spectrum of colours.

The seemingly fragile, iridescent bubble of the
FL/Y pendant lamp exploits the ethereal quality of
transparent methacrylate plastic. The oversized shade
shields the bulb and disperses a pool of light, while
the plastic reduces glare and produces a tinted glow.
Available in a spectrum of colours, the shades can be
combined in clusters to create areas of different hues
where their outlines overlap. The playful combination
of form and material lends the product a pop sensibility,
and its versatility has made it a popular fixture in bar
and restaurant interiors, as well as in residential projects
where a subtle injection of character is required.
    Italian designer Ferruccio Laviani came to
international prominence when he was invited to be
part of an exhibition by the radical Memphis design
collective in 1986. He took control of the creative
direction at Italian design brand Kartell in 1991 and
has since overseen the development of its portfolio
of products, which focuses on innovative and iconic
designs in plastic.

⌐   The shades can be
hung in groups to enhance
their chromatic contrast.

Product	Designer	Manufacturer	Date
Blossom	**Tord Boontje**	**Swarovski**	**2002**

Blossom is a contemporary reinterpretation of the traditional cut crystal chandelier that incorporates LED light sources to illuminate the faceted surfaces of hundreds of Swarovski crystals. The chandelier's overtly romantic and organic form is characteristic of Dutch designer Tord Boontje and his ability to transform unexpected materials into expressions of nature using cutting-edge techniques. The light sources are surrounded by arrangements of crystals, resembling blossoms sprouting from a branch, that are programmed to blink on and off sequentially, creating a glittering effect.

Blossom was part of the first collection commissioned by crystal manufacturer Swarovski for its Swarovski Crystal Palace exhibition at the Milan Furniture Fair in 2002. It was presented alongside other chandeliers designed by Hella Jongerius, Paola Navone, Georg Badele and Nigel Coates. The designers were challenged with 'reinventing the chandelier' using the materials and expertise provided by the Austrian company, which continues to encourage designers to explore the relationship between lighting, art and design through an ongoing programme of projects and exhibitions.

< Blossom resembles a
branch swathed in clusters
of sparkling crystal flowers.

∧ Two hundred and forty
white LED light sources
are concealed among
the crystal decorations.

Product
Family Lamp

Designer
Atelier Van Lieshout

Manufacturer
Carpenters Workshop Gallery

Date
2007

‹   Family Lamp portrays a group of faceless figures that belong to Atelier Van Lieshout's dystopian Slave City project.

⌐ The forms melt into one another, creating a stable base for the light fitting and oversized shade.

The dark and disturbing presence of Family Lamp is typical of Dutch designer Joep Van Lieshout's work, which often involves macabre and distorted interpretations of the human form. The faceless life-size family is characteristic of a leitmotif Van Lieshout developed for his ongoing Slave City project. This project imagines a dystopian scenario in which humans are contained in a fictional 'concentration camp' and treated as anonymous workers joined in a functional mass that must generate profit or face being recycled as fuel.

Constructed from reinforced fibreglass, the crude forms feature an irregular surface texture that Van Lieshout first developed in the early 1980s when he began creating sculptural objects from brightly coloured polyester. A light fixture on the top of the largest figure's head is shielded by an oversized cylindrical shade, reminiscent of the fabric diffusers found on traditional standing lamps. Van Lieshout's unique or limited edition functional sculptures traverse the line between design and art and are widely exhibited in galleries and at international fairs.

Product
Light Blubs

Designer
Pieke Bergmans

Date
2008

∧   The Light Blubs are
made from mouth-blown
crystal glass that seems
to drip from the fittings.

∧   The bulbs take their form from the surfaces they attach themselves to.

Light Blubs is part of an ongoing project by Dutch designer Pieke Bergmans, based on integrating principles of mutability and viral behavior with everyday objects. The 'virus' first manifested itself in her 2007 Crystal Virus series, which consisted of mouth-blown glass vessels pressed onto pieces of furniture so the molten glass scorched the surfaces and flowed over the edges. Bergmans was subsequently invited by German design brand Vitra to apply the same technique to some of its famous products, which became the 'hosts' for the parasitic glass shapes.

At the Milan Furniture Fair in 2008, Bergmans applied the concept to familiar lighting products, transforming conventional light bulbs into oozing protuberances that surrender to the pull of gravity or coagulate on redundant pieces of office furniture, such as a filing cabinet rendered superfluous by digital storage systems. LED light sources inside the bulbs help them to retain a semblance of their original functionality. Using the mass-produced incandescent bulb as a starting point, the implementation of an unpredictable process results in unique pieces that adapt to their surroundings.

Product
Titanic Lamp

Designer
Charles Trevelyan

Date
2005

∧ Titanic Lamp seems to
be sinking into the surface
on which it's placed.

A traditional table lamp is given a playful twist by Australian designer Charles Trevelyan, who developed this piece as a personal project following his studies in materials engineering and three-dimensional design. The lathed wood base and fabric shade are sliced at an angle so the lamp appears to be sinking into the surface on which it rests. A visual one-liner that references the ill-fated cruise ship *RMS Titanic* in its form and title, the product is typical of a twenty-first century trend for witty products based on archetypal forms.

Titanic Lamp was conceived as an artistic statement rather than as a function-led design and was initially available as an edition from Carpenters Workshop Gallery, for whom Trevelyan has also developed several other larger sculptural lighting pieces. Trevelyan went on to cofound the award-winning furniture and product design consultancy, Viable, which has seen pieces brought to market by brands including Habitat and Decode.

❮   The simple act of
slicing the base and shade
at an angle creates a witty
visual illusion.

Product	Designer	Manufacturer	Date
Bourgie	**Ferruccio Laviani**	**Kartell**	**2004**

❮ Bourgie reinterprets the ornate hand-carved ornamentation of the Baroque period in contemporary moulded polycarbonate.

‹ Light catches the
scrolled edges of the base
and is refracted by the
pleated shade.

Originally produced to showcase the flawless clarity
of transparent polycarbonate, Bourgie's playful form
evokes the intricate detailing of classic Baroque
designs. The plastic's reflective properties lend the
lamp the appearance of cut crystal, reinforcing the
impression of inherent preciousness despite its being
made from a relatively inexpensive and robust
material. The title is an abbreviated version of the
French word 'bourgeoisie' and enhances the product's
ironic take on the idea of luxury.

A tripod base formed from three identical parts
incorporates a sophisticated attachment system that
allows the shade to be set at three different heights
for use on a variety of surfaces. Matt black and white
versions are produced in batch-dyed polycarbonate,
and Kartell introduced more extravagant chrome and
gold-plated ABS plastic variations to supplement the
range. The lamp's iconoclastic design – combining
formal references from a previous era with
contemporary materials – enables it to sit comfortably
alongside antiques and objects of varying aesthetic
styles, making it a popular choice for use in modern
or eclectic interiors.

Product	Designer	Manufacturer	Date
Skygarden	**Marcel Wanders**	**Flos**	**2007**

L Skygarden's die-cast aluminium alloy exterior contrasts with the traditional ornamentation on the inner surface.

When the light source inside this pendant shade is switched on, it reveals a decorative frieze of flowers, leaves and ribbons on the internal surface. Dutch designer Marcel Wanders was inspired by the ornate plasterwork covering the ceiling of his former home, and the product replicates its classical aesthetic on a smaller and more portable scale. When viewed from directly underneath, the circular frieze resembles an ornamental ceiling rose from which a chandelier or light fitting would traditionally have been suspended.

The light source is contained within a flash-blown opal glass diffuser capped with a steel plate. A filigree pattern etched into the steel adds an extra layer of decoration. The hemispherical shade's simple, unadorned exterior creates a deliberate contrast with the decadent decoration concealed within. This juxtaposition of contemporary and traditional styles is symptomatic of the playful postmodern approach favoured by Wanders and many of his peers (see also Jurgen Bey, pages 100 and 101, Ferruccio Laviani, pages 017, 044, 045, 054 and 055, and Charles Trevelyan, pages 052 and 053).

∧   The hemispherical shade's interior is decorated with a frieze inspired by a plasterwork ceiling.

Product
Gun Lamp

Designer
Philippe Starck

Manufacturer
Flos

Date
2005

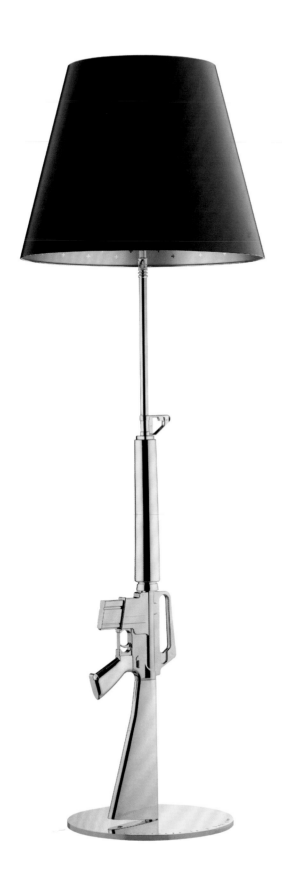

L The Gun Lamps
symbolise the relationship
between violence and our
contemporary commodity-
driven culture.

∨ The lamps are
cast in aluminium from
replica weapons.

Philippe Starck's provocative Gun Lamps are intended
to symbolise the violence that exists in modern society
and is exacerbated by rampant consumerism and a
commodity-driven culture. The replicas of a Beretta
pistol, a Kalashnikov and an M16 rifle are cast in
aluminium and finished in 18-carat gold or chrome
plate to evoke the look of money and its destructive
power. The matt black or white plasticised paper
shade features a silkscreen pattern of crosses on the
inside to represent death and an inscription around
the circumference of the base reads 'Happiness is
a hot gun'.

　　The decision to confront consumers with a replica
of a deadly weapon transformed into a harmless everyday
object reflects Starck's famed self-confidence and
aptitude for publicity. A commission based on sales
of the Kalashnikov model is paid to the inventor of the
original gun – who never received royalties for his design
– while a donation is also made to the humanitarian aid
organisation Médecins Sans Frontiers.

Product	Designer	Manufacturer	Date
Pigeon Light	**Ed Carpenter**	**Thorsten van Elten**	**2001**

L   The Pigeon Light was
designed as an alternative
urban souvenir.

Ed Carpenter originally trained as a sculptor at
Kingston University before working on independent
furniture and interior design projects and eventually
enrolling on the Design Products course at the Royal
College of Art. As part of his coursework, Carpenter
was challenged to design an 'urban souvenir', and
chose to celebrate the humble pigeon as an alternative
icon of London and an antidote to the quaint ceramic
figurines of farmyard animals that can be found in
many British homes.

A batch of roughly 100 lamps made from vacuum-
formed plastic for his graduation show quickly sold
out, encouraging Carpenter to continue producing the
lights to order until retailer Thorsten van Elten selected
it as one of the flagship products for the launch of his
eponymous design brand. Produced from perspex
in a range of colours with a beech stand and clothes
peg foot, the product's quirky form and 'ready-made'
materials have made it a popular low-budget
statement design.

Carpenter continues to work independently on
design projects for clients, including Established &
Sons, Authentics and Modus, and formed a partnership
with German designer André Klauser, with whom he
collaborates on design projects under the name
Klauser & Carpenter.

L   A clothes peg foot allows
the light to be attached to
a wall-mounted stand.

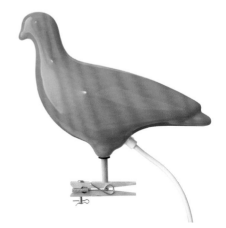

Product
Animal Lamps

Designer
Front

Manufacturer
Moooi

Date
2006

L   Life-size casts of animals
fitted with lights create a
surprising centrepiece.

∨   The horse stands over
two metres high, while the
rabbit can perch on the
floor or a table.

When Swedish design collective Front were invited
to design a bar area at the Stockholm Furniture Fair in
2006, they created a fantastical scenography featuring
furnishings made mostly from existing objects. They
spray-painted garden ornaments in the shape of
life-size animals and added tray surfaces to transform
them into tables on which visitors could place drinks
and snacks. Giant cushions and tables on wheels added
to the surreal tableaux.

Despite being intended for one-time use at the
event, the animals captured the attention of Dutch
design brand Moooi, who helped to develop them for
production. A light source and lampshade were added
to the horse, which is now the most iconic of the
original furnishings, often appearing in the lobbies
of trendy hotels and restaurants. A rabbit table lamp
and a side table shaped as a pig complete the family.

The animals are moulded from black polyester,
and a cotton lampshade with a PVC interior directs
light onto their features. The products helped bring
Front – who were known for their conceptual projects –
to the attention of an international design audience and
led to commissions from companies including IKEA,
Kartell and Skitsch.

Product	Designer	Manufacturer	Date
Dear Ingo	**Ron Gilad**	**Moooi**	**2003**

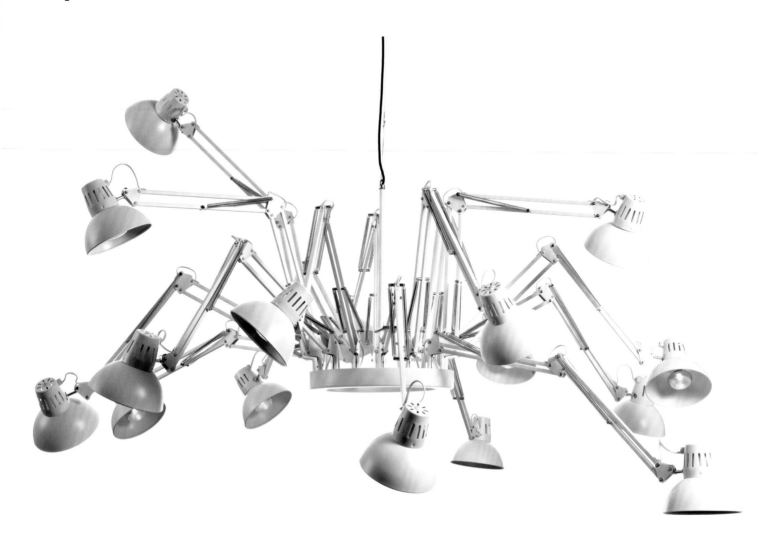

L   Sixteen articulated
lamps arranged around
a central ring can be
individually adjusted
to direct the light.

∨   The product's title pays
homage to Gilad's friend
and mentor, Ingo Maurer.

Ron Gilad's spider-like chandelier is made up of 16
individual articulated lamps that emerge from a central
ring and can be raised, lowered or rotated to direct
light in whichever way is required. Functionality,
however, is not the main concern of Gilad's sculptural
creation, which demands attention, as well as plenty
of space, and is typical of his playful portfolio.
     Gilad studied industrial design at Jerusalem's
Bezalel Academy of Art and Design and taught 3D
design at the Shenkar College of Engineering and
Design in Ramat Gan, Israel, before moving to New
York, where his first studio was situated above a shop
belonging to German lighting designer Ingo Maurer.
Dear Ingo was created as an homage to Maurer's
whimsical ready-made lighting designs. The original
version was made using task lights from IKEA, but
Dutch design firm Moooi developed the product to be
manufactured from custom-made powder-coated steel
parts. The amusing re-appropriation and multiplication
of a familiar utilitarian object invokes standardisation
and mass manufacture, while the spoked form
references the branches of traditional chandeliers.

Product	Designer	Manufacturer	Date
Garland	**Tord Boontje**	**Habitat/Artecnica**	**2002**

‹ Garland is made from
a thin metal sheet etched
with a delicate pattern of
foliage and flowers.

∧ The product arrives
flat and is manipulated
by the user so it drapes
around the light bulb.

This seminal piece by Dutch product designer Tord
Boontje marked a turning point in his career and
coincided with a significant shift within the discipline
of interior design towards more delicate and decorative
forms. Previously, Boontje – who studied at Design
Academy Eindhoven and then at the Royal College
of Art, where he returned as a tutor in 2002 – had
been creating low-tech, low-cost products, which
often incorporated existing objects. An interest in
nature and the intense sensuality and richness of
hand-crafted objects from previous centuries provoked
a switch to the gentler and more sensual style for
which he is best known.

The product was originally presented as part
of Boontje's 'Wednesday' collection, which included
furniture and glassware decorated with patterns and
iconography inspired by nature. This initial version
was made from stainless steel but the product was
developed for production in lighter brass by British
brand Habitat. Garland arrives as a flat sheet of
precisely etched flowers and leaves that the user
bends and twists around a naked bulb so the strands
surround the light and cast delicate shadows. The
product's playful and customisable form led to it
becoming a popular alternative to more conventional,
rigid lighting products.

Product	Designer	Manufacturer	Date
Caboche	**Patricia Urquiola** **and Eliana Gerotto**	**Foscarini**	**2005**

Clear plastic beads covering the surface of Caboche replicate the aesthetic of opulent crystal chandeliers.

The form of Caboche was inspired by the designers' desire to recapture the timeless appeal of chandeliers made from strings of crystal beads. An initial prototype consisted of a metal structure covered in glass spheres, but this solution proved heavy and expensive, so the designers created a framework from transparent thermoplastic and covered this in beads made from the same material. The transparent or gold-tinted spheres help disperse the light and act like lenses, reflecting and multiplying their surroundings.

A metal ring at the top holds the light fitting and curving plastic ribs join this ring to the base, creating a bulbous skeleton onto which the spheres are clipped in uniform rows. A satinised blown glass diffuser helps produce an even light and reduces glare. The use of a transparent material enables the lamp to disappear into the background when turned off and assume a jewel-like radiance when illuminated.

^ The elegant shape and construction has been applied to floor, table and pendant variations.

Product	Designer	Manufacturer	Date
Booklamp	**Seyhan Özdemir and Sefer Çağlar/ Autoban**	**De La Espada**	**2006**

L Booklamp combines a diffused light source with a useful surface for resting a book.

¬ The product is manufactured in several types of solid wood or from high-density fibreboard.

Booklamp responds to the everyday scenario of reading a book at bedtime in a poetic and practical way by combining the function of a bedside lamp with a handy surface for storing reading material. The simple lines and tapered legs of the solid wood stand are reminiscent of elegant mid-century furniture, while the tall fabric shade evokes traditional floor-standing lamps. A curved top surface and disproportionate shade add character to an otherwise straightforward product.

Istanbul studio Autoban was founded in 2003 by Seyhan Özdemir and Sefer Çağlar. The pair met as students in Istanbul, Turkey, where Özdemir was studying architecture and Çağlar was studying interior design. After gaining several years of experience in their respective disciplines, they began collaborating on interior design projects before expanding into product design and architecture. Booklamp is typical of Autoban's playful sensibility and respect for honest, authentic materials and fine craftsmanship. The product is manufactured by specialist woodworkers in the Portuguese factory of design brand De La Espada.

Product	Designer	Manufacturer	Date
Tab	**Barber Osgerby**	**Flos**	**2007**

L Tab's simple folded diffuser shields the bulb from view and helps to direct the light.

❯ The protruding tab on the top of the shade can be used to adjust the angle of the diffuser.

British design studio Barber Osgerby uses a simple fold in the die-cast aluminium shade of this lamp to channel the light and eliminate glare. Radiused edges give the product an approachable aesthetic, and the eponymous tab that protrudes from the top of the shade clearly signals the point of contact for adjusting and swivelling the shade.

In the early years of their collaboration, Edward Barber and Jay Osgerby favoured folded forms that could be produced from sheet material, as they were familiar with this technique from making card models while studying architecture at the Royal College of Art. Tab is a return to this simple method of generating form and epitomises the function-led, exploratory approach that the pair are renowned for. The lamp deliberately defies archetypes traditionally associated with task lighting, resulting in a product that is unencumbered by precedents and has a timeless simplicity.

Product
Piani

Designer
**Ronan and Erwan
Bouroullec**

Manufacturer
Flos

Date
2011

L An LED spotlight
illuminates the contents
of the container below.

French brothers Ronan and Erwan Bouroullec are
renowned for creating products that respond to
everyday scenarios in intelligent ways through
the refined application of form and materials. This
table lamp does just that by incorporating a useful
receptacle for miscellaneous objects like keys,
spectacles or coins. A ring of LEDs in the upper section
projects light downwards, highlighting the simple stem
that joins the horizontal elements and illuminating
the accoutrements below. The two-tiered design is
produced in ABS plastic, with oak and basalt versions
offering a more tactile alternative.

    The Bouroullec brothers came to prominence at
the Milan Furniture Fair in 2000, where Italian brand
Cappellini presented their design for a platform bed
enclosed in a plywood and soldered steel structure.
They continue to collaborate with many of the world's
leading manufacturers on projects that challenge
conventional ideas about how products should look
and perform, seeking out new functionalities suited
to modern lifestyles.

∧   A recessed tray
provides storage space
for small everyday objects.

The humble light bulb is celebrated in this simple and playful product by Swedish designer Mattias Ståhlbom, who had the idea after he observed friends creating ad hoc lighting solutions by combining naked bulbs with rudimentary electrical components. A long silicone rubber cord ends in an elegantly proportioned socket for a standard E27 bulb, which is left to hang uncovered. The cords have a strong graphic aesthetic and can be suspended individually, in clusters or in rows. A wide spectrum of available colours makes the product extremely versatile.

Mattias Ståhlbom is a partner at Stockholm-based architecture and design studio TAF, whose projects address everyday objects and experiences from a humorous and rational standpoint. E27 exemplifies Ståhlbom's dedication to simple design with a whimsical approach to detail and materials. The product required a rigorous process of refinement to determine the ideal proportions and surface textures for the cord and socket. E27 honours the familiar aesthetic of electricity – of extension cords, fuses and sockets – and offers an affordable yet sophisticated alternative to traditional pendant shades.

∧ This simple product consists of a long silicone cord and socket that houses a standard E27 bulb.

˥ The cords can be draped across the ceiling or walls or hung in clusters.

Product
Maki

Designer
Nendo

Manufacturer
Foscarini

Date
2011

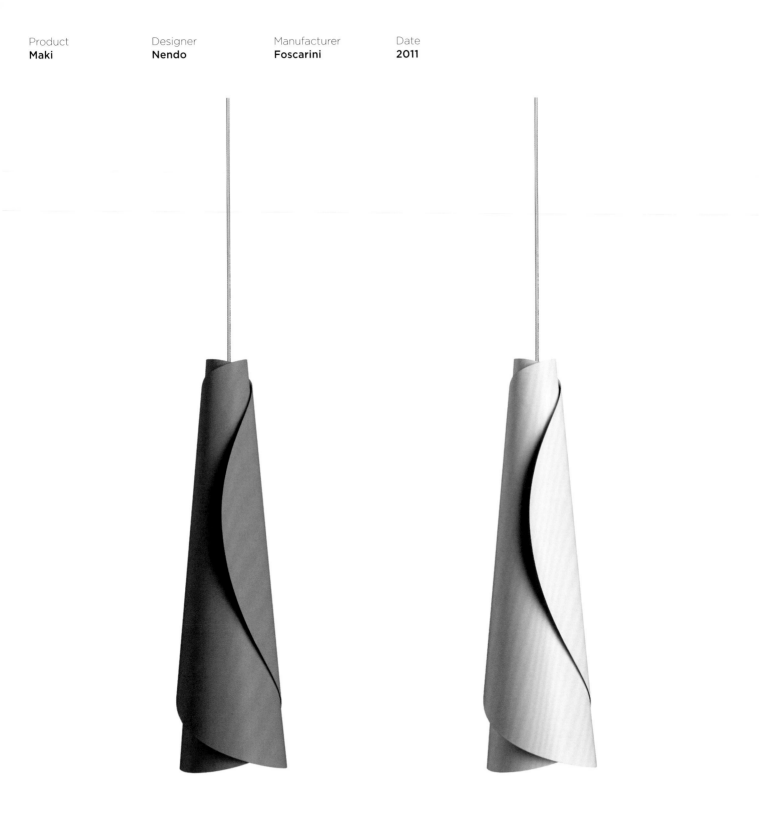

⌐ Maki is made by combining two rolled sheets of aluminium.

⌐ The bulb is completely hidden, adding to the impression that the surfaces themselves are glowing.

'Maki' means 'to roll something' in Japanese, and it is this act that provides the basis for Japanese design studio Nendo's pendant shade. The design process began with the simple gesture of rolling a circular sheet of paper to produce a conical form. Two such forms slot together to create a shade that resembles the spiralling shape of a seashell. Nendo's chief designer Oki Sato wanted to create a product that provides different kinds of light, and Maki achieves this by emitting a strong directional beam from the base of the shade, while a subtler diffused glow emanates from the gaps between the two cones.

Aluminium was chosen for the shell, as Sato felt it would offer a result similar to the original paper models. Before the sheets are rolled, a hole is cut to increase the amount of light that reaches the edges. These holes become invisible when the two parts are combined. Maki's design typifies Sato's ethos: to create simple products that elegantly and straightforwardly combine form and materials to communicate a singular idea.

Product
Ge-Off Sphere

Designer
Ron Arad

Date
2000

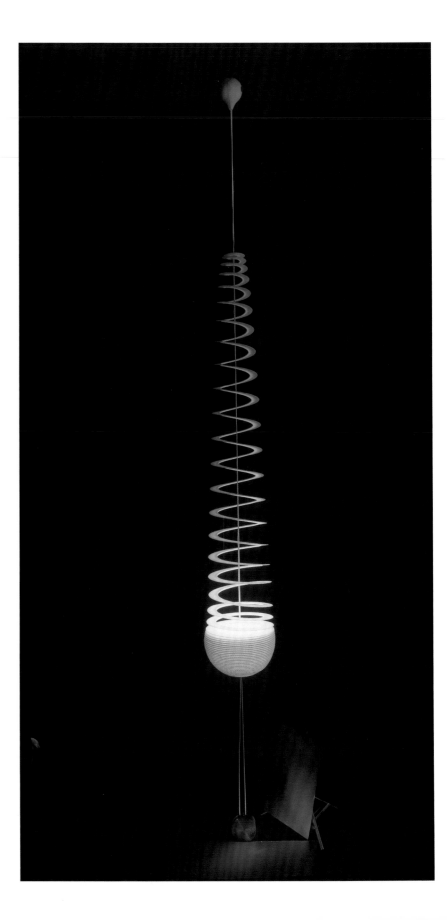

In 2000, Ron Arad developed a collection of products using 3D printing technologies, an emerging technique used by automotive and mechanical engineers to rapidly produce complex models or prototype parts. Arad's fascination with this computerised manufacturing process led him to design a series of sculptural pieces exploring the potential for mass-produced products that require minimal human input.

Titled, 'Not Made by Hand, Not Made in China', the collection includes several items based on a handwritten copy of this titular phrase, which is extruded and manipulated using computer software to create three-dimensional forms. These are then printed and assigned functions such as jewellery, vessels and other products. The spiralling shape of the Ge-Off Sphere lamp accommodates a light source in the base to highlight the delicacy of the structure as it stretches up the cord. Text running around the spiralling surface adds a poetic element and exploits the accuracy of the process. Arad's experiments were among the earliest to show how this advanced technology could facilitate the manufacture of forms that would have previously seemed impossible to produce.

< The spiralling form is printed from layers of polyamide plastic powder.

L Handwriting included in the surface demonstrates the precision that can be achieved by digital manufacturing.

Product
LILY.MGX

Designer
Janne Kyttanen

Manufacturer
Materialise.MGX

Date
2003

← LILY.MGX is an early example of a product designed to be made using additive manufacturing technologies.

⌐ A central light source illuminates the delicate petals, which are arranged in a layered configuration.

LILY.MGX is manufactured using an additive layering process that enables forms created in three-dimensional software packages to be printed in incremental layers from a plastic powder. The lamp was developed by Finnish designer Janne Kyttanen during his studies at the Gerrit Rietveld Academy in Amsterdam. The design received support from Belgian company Materialise, which specialises in the production of objects using additive manufacturing.

The lampshade was one of several pieces presented by Materialise (under their .MGX label) at the Milan Furniture Fair in 2004 to draw attention to potential consumer applications for their emerging technologies. Its precise organic form, which elegantly exploits the cutting-edge manufacturing method, earned it a Red Dot Award in 2005 and a place in the permanent collections of both New York's Museum of Arts and Design and Helsinki's DESIGNMUSEO.

Materialise has collaborated with numerous designers to develop innovative products that emphasise the delicate and complex forms enabled by additive manufacturing processes. Lighting designs are particularly well suited to this technique, as the commonly used polyester-based materials can produce unusual shapes, textures and attractive shadows.

Product
Attracted to Light

Designer
Geoffrey Mann

Date
2005

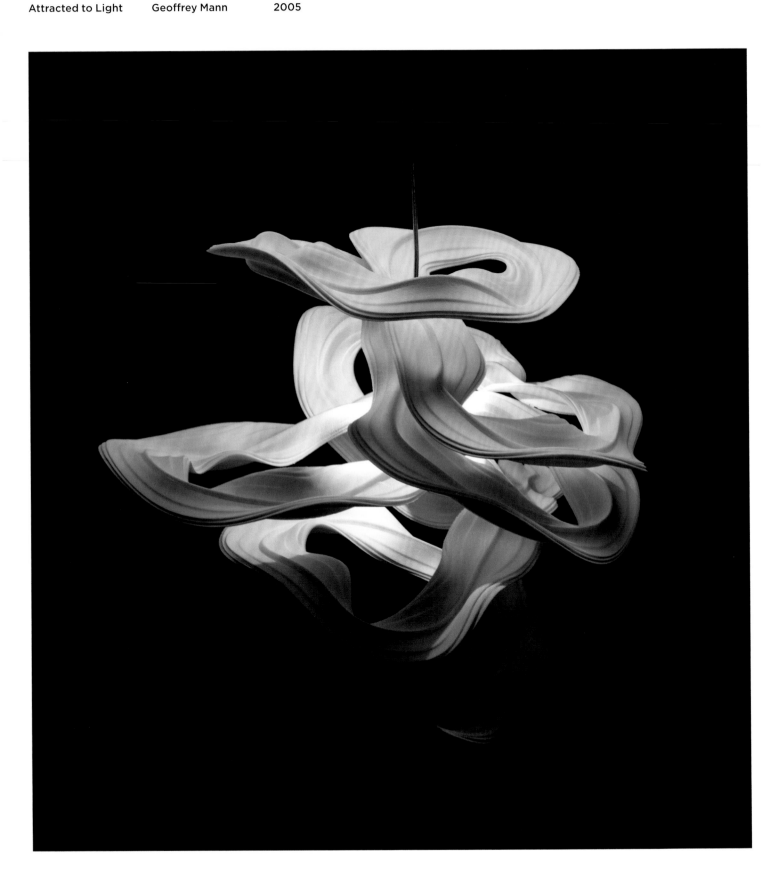

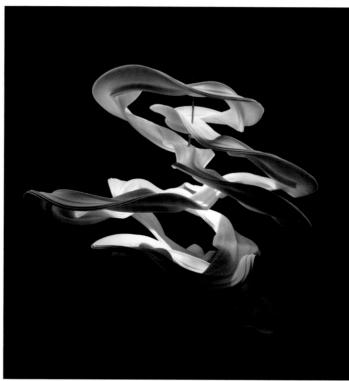

∧ The twisting form of this sculptural pendant shade traces the erratic flight path of a moth around a light bulb.

⌐ Adding a light source helps to bring context to the form, which from certain angles takes on the conical outline of a lampshade.

While studying ceramics and glass at the Royal College of Art, Scottish artist and designer Geoffrey Mann became interested in the possibility of immortalising moments in time and ephemeral traces, such as the erratic path of a moth circling a light source. Using sophisticated three-dimensional recording equipment, he captured the trajectory of a moth within the confines of a lampshade and translated this data into a digital representation of the moth's movements.

The resulting computer model is fed into a 3D printer that builds the form from a polyamide plastic resembling porcelain or bone china. Only a small number of pieces have been made due to the expensive processes involved. The unique form of each light is a consequence of different sections of the recorded data being used as the basis for the model: the longer the chosen period, the more dense and complex the shape becomes. The silhouette of a moth can be seen in the section of the spiralling ribbon-like form.

Product
Fall of the Damned

Designer
Luc Merx

Manufacturer
Gagat international

Date
2007

‹ Fall of the
Damned combines
historical iconography
with contemporary
manufacturing techniques.

⌐ The chandelier's
detailed form is printed
from a computer-generated
file using an additive layer
fabrication process.

The dense accumulation of twisting bodies that
make up this chandelier by Dutch architect and
designer Luc Merx could be produced using only
cutting-edge additive layer fabrication. Arranged in
concentric rings, each of the figures touches several
others so no additional structural elements are
required. The digital model is printed using a selective
laser sintering process that builds the shape gradually
in layers, achieving an extremely fine resolution.
     The light's narrative form references a seventeenth
century religious painting by Peter Paul Rubens, which
shows the bodies of the damned toppling into the
abyss. The dramatic chiaroscuro effect in the painting
is evoked in Merx's design by the contrast between
the brightly illuminated figures closest to the light
source and those on the periphery, which are cast
in shadows by the mass of limbs. Fall of the Damned
is part of a larger research project in which Merx's
practice, Gagat international, adapts historical
iconography to explore the formal freedom afforded
by new manufacturing techniques.

Materials

< 28 series
Omer Arbel's glass
pendant shades
demonstrate how classic
materials and handcrafted
processes can still be used
to create spectacular
lighting products.

Light brings the best out of materials; enlivening the nuances of textural surfaces, enhancing colours and accentuating the intrinsic dichotomy between the immateriality of light itself and the physicality of a product's form. This section focuses on experimental and innovative uses for materials that deliberately avoid or challenge established typologies and respond to changing social and environmental trends. Since the introduction of electric lighting, bases for floor and table lamps have typically been made from wood or cast metal, with fabric shades diffusing the light. Similarly, fabric is commonly used for ceiling-hung pendant shades, while chandeliers decorated with crystal beads have been popular since the days of candlelight. Although these familiar materials continue to dominate popular lighting design, the abundance of traditional and contemporary materials available to twenty-first century designers provides an irresistible opportunity to explore new ways of celebrating the reflective, refractive and diffusive properties of light.

For many contemporary designers, materials provide the starting point for their creative process. In the 1980s, designers such as Ron Arad and Tom Dixon became renowned for their inventive products made from cheap materials like welded metal and found objects. This materials-led design approach influenced a successive generation of creative talent, including British designer Benjamin Hubert, who describes the output of his studio as 'Materials Driven. Process Led. Industrial Design'. Hubert's projects focus on exploring the technical and aesthetic properties of innovative or unusual materials. His lighting designs include a series of delicate diffusers made from fabrics usually used to produce sportswear and underwear (Tenda, 2012), and a concrete shade that belies the material's weight (Heavy Light, 2008-09). Designers like Hubert constantly seek out materials and processes they can adapt for new purposes, and lighting provides a suitable format for exploiting the functional and aesthetic qualities of these materials.

The development of new materials for use in other industries also inspires and facilitates innovation in lighting design. Almost any material can be used to direct or diffuse light, and properties such as density, texture and colour offer opportunities to produce interesting forms or effects. Austrian designer Marc Sadler's Mite and Tite lamps were informed by his experience of designing ski boots using lightweight composite materials. He spent two years developing a composite of fibreglass and Kevlar®, or carbon thread, which is used to produce slender and delicate diffusers that are strong enough to support themselves. The surprising behaviour of the Hanabi light, by Oki Sato of Japanese studio Nendo, results from the appropriation of a material normally used in the aeronautical and automotive industries. Strips of shape-memory alloy – a metal that reverts back to its cold-forged shape when heated – are arranged around the light source and fan out when heat from the bulb warms the metal. Such cutting-edge materials offer twenty-first century designers extraordinary opportunities to create poetic forms and experiences that supplement the functionality of light.

While some designers focus on finding innovative applications for new materials, others are content to revisit materials that have been synonymous with lighting for hundreds of years. Jasper Morrison's Glo-Ball is an icon of modern lighting design, with a diffuser made from familiar milky-white opal glass. The entire surface of Glo-Ball's acid-etched diffuser seems to glow when the bulb is illuminated, producing a soft, even light that gives the product a timeless appeal. Morrison's ability to identify the essence of a material and create a refined form that enables light itself to become the focus of attention results in an extremely versatile and popular lamp.

Traditionally, coloured glass is associated with stained glass windows and use in decorative lamps that accentuate the material's translucency. Contemporary designers continue to exploit the intriguing aesthetic properties of glass, which enables combinations of form and colour to create overlapping areas of blended hues, with reflections adding an extra visual dimension. Light Tray, by Norwegian designers Andreas Engesvik and Daniel Rybakken, is a modern reinterpretation of a table lamp that exhibits all of these qualities. Domes of coloured glass can be arranged in any configuration to cover bulbs that emerge from a flat rectangular surface, creating new hues where the colours overlap. The product demonstrates that designers are still able to identify new ways to create spectacular and original applications for one of the oldest materials found in lighting design.

Paper is another material that has been used for centuries to diffuse light. Paper lanterns play an important role in traditional Japanese and Chinese festivals, as well as in Hispanic Christmas celebrations. The material's thickness and texture allow light to penetrate; creating a soft, flickering glow when combined with candlelight or a steady, warm light when used as a shade for a conventional bulb. The iconic Akari series of sculptural paper shades created by Japanese-American designer Isamu Noguchi in 1951 captured the essence of typical Japanese bamboo and paper lanterns, and set a precedent for subsequent paper lights that have become popular in Western interiors. However, paper can be applied to lighting products using other forms and methods that exploit not only its aesthetic but also its structural and sustainable credentials. American designer Victor Vetterlein's cartoonish Trash Me VV1 lamp is made from a moulded paper pulp similar to that used for throwaway packaging. Swedish studio Claesson Koivisto Rune collaborated with a forestry agency on the design of an LED task light made from laminated biodegradable wood pulp that has excellent structural strength when folded. By combining sustainable materials, such as paper, with efficient technologies and contemporary production methods, designers are able to create stylish and innovative lighting products with improved ecological credentials.

The influence of sustainability on design has increased since the beginning of the twenty-first century, as designers and manufacturers are forced to respond to a greater societal awareness of ecological concerns. As well as adjusting to energy-saving light

sources, consumers have begun to consider factors such as the provenance and sustainable merit of materials when buying new products. This has led to a renewed interest in craftsmanship and the manufacture of products using locally available resources or waste material. Within lighting, the trend for reconditioning unwanted objects – often referred to as 'upcycling' – has yielded several significant examples. Stuart Haygarth's chandelier made from assorted scraps of plastic washed up on a beach and Lee Broom's early collections combining light sources with found objects – including furniture and vintage decanters – focus on the beauty that exists in objects that already have their own history. Although these projects represent artistic statements rather than genuine attempts to reduce landfill, they promote a degree of introspection regarding design's role in the profligate consumption of the world's diminishing resources.

As the development of energy-efficient lighting technologies continues to gather pace, it is inevitable that designers are concurrently attempting to reduce the amount of material used in their products' manufacture. The negligible size and weight of LEDs in comparison to conventional bulbs, for example, means they can be combined with similarly lightweight materials, as the need for structural support is greatly reduced. The delicate sculptural structures used to create the Fragile Future family of chandeliers and wall and table lights by Dutch design duo Lonneke Gordijn and Ralph Nauta typify the ethereal products that such technologies enable. Three-dimensional modules made from thin strips of phosphorous bronze carry a current to LEDs, which are covered in dandelion seeds to suggest a symbiosis between nature and technology. Combining efficient light sources with unnecessarily hefty materials makes little ecological sense, so the

‹ Tenda
Benjamin Hubert focuses
on finding innovative
applications for new
materials, such as the
high-tech fabrics employed
in his Tenda collection.

evolution of more lightweight and sustainable lighting products seems a logical progression.

The next step in the reductive trend to minimise lighting's physical presence is already under way, and the focus has switched from the materials used to make products to those used to manufacture the light sources themselves. Experiments with light-emitting organic compounds have resulted in materials that can be used to create paper-thin luminous surfaces, such as those found in OLED panels and electroluminescent films. Although not yet sufficiently powerful to act as primary light sources, prototypal applications for these materials preface the development of luminous surfaces that could change the way lighting products are designed and manufactured. New York designer Marcus Tremonto's innovative and irreverent Hexalights, for example, resemble two-dimensional drawings of six-sided shapes and are printed on sheets of electroluminescent material that glows gently when a current is applied. These materials need time to mature, but the pressure to reduce the amounts of energy and resources we consume will ensure that their development will be significantly incentivised and rewarded.

The refinement of light-emitting surfaces that produce an evenly diffused luminescence could signal the end for the traditional combination of a point light source and diffuser. These materials can be integrated into surfaces or products and applied to forms that achieve an omnidirectional ambient light, much like an incandescent bulb. In the face of such changes, glass, fabric, paper and other materials typically used to diffuse and reflect light become functionally redundant and will therefore take on an increasingly decorative or nostalgic role. Although these materials may no longer be required to diffuse light, their familiar and comforting colours, textures and patina have an intrinsic appeal that transcends functionality. Designers must use materials intelligently to augment the benefits of new light sources while maintaining the important tangible relationship that exists between people and lighting products.

Product
Tide

Designer
Stuart Haygarth

Date
2004

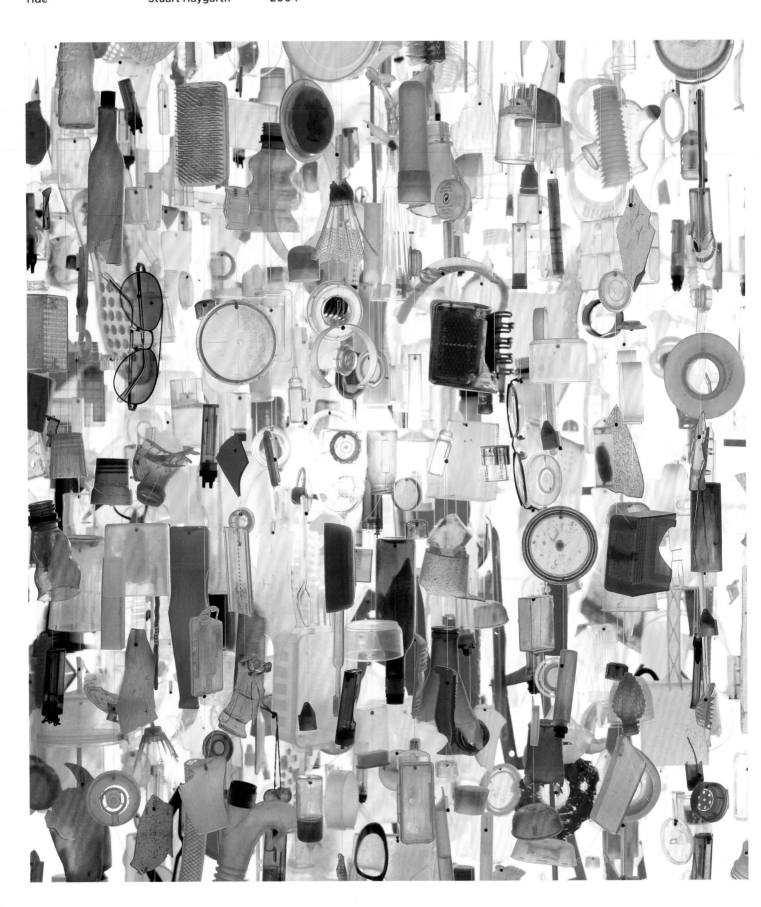

< Random items
washed up on a beach are
suspended around a bulb
to form a colourful sphere.

⌐ The imposing yet
ethereal chandelier has
a diameter of 150cm.

Over a period of several years, British designer
Stuart Haygarth went for walks with his dog along
the beaches of the south coast of England and
accumulated a curious collection of man-made debris
that had washed up on the shore. The Tide chandelier
consists of hundreds of these discarded and weathered
pieces of flotsam and jetsam arranged in a spherical
array around a single 100-watt incandescent bulb.
Predominantly made of plastic, the translucent and
transparent objects refract light in colourful patterns.
Each element is painstakingly attached to a monofilament
line and suspended from a square platform. The resulting
sphere evokes the shape of the moon, whose force
created the tide that washed these items ashore.

Haygarth spent 15 years working as a photographic
illustrator, which helped him gain an appreciation for
the properties of light and colour. Tide was his first
divergence into the world of three-dimensional design
and has since been succeeded by several similar pieces,
including chandeliers made from party-poppers
(Millennium, 2004), spectacle lenses (Spectacle, 2006)
and coloured vehicle lights (Tail Light, 2007), all of
which transform broken, banal and unwanted objects
into limited-edition sculptures that celebrate light.

Product
Ruminant Bloom

Designer
Julia Lohmann

Date
2004

‹ Preserved cow and sheep stomachs are transformed into lamps that highlight the richly textured surfaces.

⌐ The products encourage us to consider potential uses for the parts of animals that are usually discarded.

For her graduation project from the Royal College of Art, German designer Julia Lohmann produced lamps made from preserved cow and sheep stomachs that confront the uncomfortable issue of what happens to waste resulting from the butchering of animals for food. Adding a light source to a material that is generally thought of as offal and discarded during meat preparation highlights the organic beauty of the delicately detailed honeycombed surfaces. Lohmann also presented a bench in the shape of a cow's torso upholstered in a whole cow skin, creating an unambiguous connection to the source of leather, which most people choose to ignore or suppress.

These projects coincided with an outbreak of art and design exploring themes of morbidity, including Polly Morgan and Kelly McCallum's sculptural taxidermy works and provocative products incorporating animal pelts by Dutch designers Niels Van Eijk and Miriam Van der Lubbe, and Wieki Somers. Lohmann's lights represent a visceral example of ready-made design that celebrates the origins of materials and communicates an alternative vision of sustainability.

Product
**Rough Diamond
collection**

Designer
Lee Broom

Manufacturer
Lee Broom

Date
2008

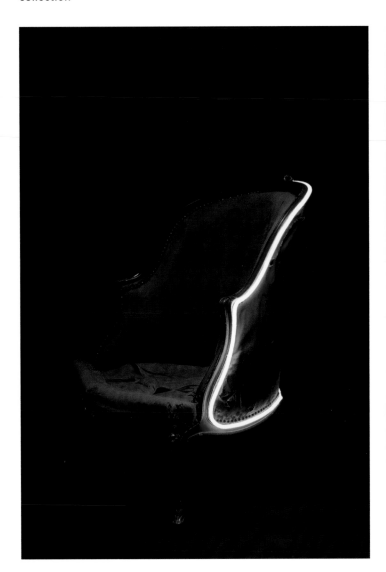

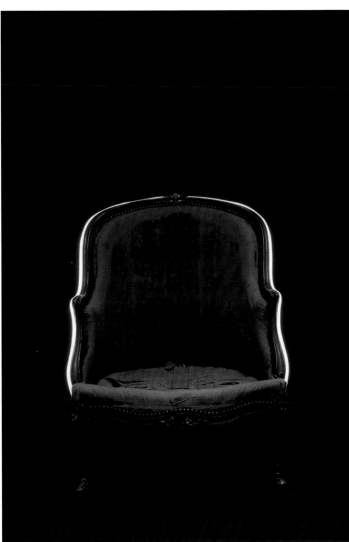

British designer Lee Broom's first furniture collection, Neo Neon, was launched during the London Design Festival in 2007 and comprised highly lacquered handmade reproductions of antique chairs, mirrors and consoles embellished with a fringe of neon to illuminate their forms. The following year, Broom released the Rough Diamond collection, this time combining found vintage furniture with lighting to create a contrast between old and new. The furniture, including an antique Bérgere chair sourced from a Paris flea market, was left unrestored, and pieces were produced in limited editions or on request.

Time spent around the bright lights of the theatre during his childhood inspired Broom's use of neon lighting in both the Neo Neon and Rough Diamond collections. Born in Birmingham in 1975, he was enrolled in theatre school at the age of seven and appeared in television and film productions until he was seventeen. Broom went on to study fashion and cofounded a successful bar design consultancy before making the transition into furniture and lighting design. The Rough Diamond collection encapsulates his enthusiasm for giving traditional objects a contemporary and theatrical makeover.

‹ The Rough Diamond collection consists of antique furniture combined with contemporary lighting.

∧ Neon tubes highlight the familiar outlines of the furniture.

Product
Light Shade Shade

Designer
Jurgen Bey

Manufacturer
Moooi

Date
1999

A traditional lamp, or crystal chandelier, is concealed behind the mirrored shade of this deceptive piece by Dutch designer Jurgen Bey. When the light is off, the one-way mirror film reflects its surroundings and hides its contents, but once illuminated the familiar form of a salvaged light fitting is revealed, evoking a bygone era that contrasts with the glossy, modern skin.

Light Shade Shade was designed for the Droog collective, with whom Bey became associated in the early 1990s. The use of found objects, which can be seen in other lighting products such as Rody Graumans' 85 Lamps chandelier (1993) and Tejo Remy's Milk Bottle Lamp (1991), was an approach favoured by the Droog designers. These conceptual works set a precedent that would inspire a successive generation of Dutch designers, including Pieke Bergmans, Maarten Baas and Studio Job. In 2002, Bey founded the Rotterdam studio Makkink & Bey with architect Rianne Makkink, which engages in experimental architecture, town planning, and interior and product design projects.

⌐ Turning on the light reveals an ornate form shielded by the slick contemporary material.

‹ A traditional lighting fixture is hidden behind a one-way mirror film.

Product	Designer	Manufacturer	Date
Decanterlight	**Lee Broom**	**Lee Broom**	**2010**

‹ Vintage cut crystal decanters are given a new purpose as lampshades.

⌐ Frosted and polished gold variations emphasise the traditional decoration in different ways.

The glittering effect of light refracting through cut crystal inspired Lee Broom to transform original lead crystal decanters into luxurious pendant shades. Having observed the proliferation of crystal decanters in flea markets and second-hand stores, Broom recognised that these objects had become largely redundant and could therefore be given a new purpose. He and his team began collecting vintage decanters, which all vary slightly in shape and size but share a common style of decoration. Adapting the decanters to their new function involves several handcrafted processes: the thick bases are carefully removed and any scuffs or scratches in the crystal are polished out before a light fitting is inserted and a traditional braided flex adds a final nostalgic detail.

Having initially focused on transforming existing objects into glamorous modern creations, Broom has shifted towards designing, manufacturing and retailing his own products. Crystal Bulb (2012), for example, is an ornamental cut crystal light bulb made by the last remaining producer of handmade English full lead crystal in the UK that evokes the sparkling pattern of the Decanterlights.

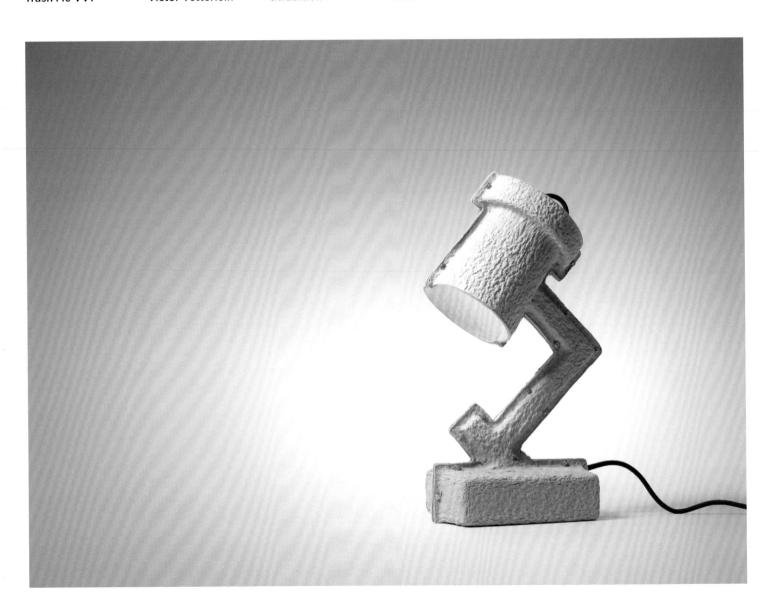

⌐ The lamp's two-part shell is made from paper pulp held together using aluminium screw posts.

⌐ A wood and concrete weight in the base has replaced the bag of bird seed that was originally used as a counterweight for the cantilevered form.

The transience of contemporary society and the ephemeral nature of many mass-produced objects inspired this lamp by American designer Victor Vetterlein. Originally made from four paper egg cartons blended with water, the product has since been developed for mass production using a standard paper pulp. The material is spread inside a mould and left to dry out and become rigid. Once the hardened form is removed from the mould a cloth-covered flex and recyclable light fitting are added.

The lamp's simple shape denotes its unusual manufacturing method and unashamedly exposes the seam that joins the two halves. The aluminium screw posts that clamp these sections together are more commonly used to bind large documents, indicating that the product can be dismantled at the end of its life and its parts reused. The straightforward assembly and application of a cheap and seemingly frail material hint at the product's inherent impermanence, while its cartoonish form and tactile surfaces give it more personality than a typical throwaway product.

Product	Designer	Manufacturer	Date
Sticky Lamp	**Chris Kabel**	**Droog**	**2002**

L Sticky Lamp gives
packaging a purpose –
just add a bulb and it's
ready to use.

> The light can be stuck
to any surface and moved
around if needed.

The packaging becomes the product in this light by Dutch designer Chris Kabel, which is ready to use once a standard E27 bulb has been attached to the fitting moulded into the plastic shell. Unlike most lighting products, which are packaged in boxes or casings that are discarded after purchase, nothing is wasted in this straightforward example of low-cost sustainable design. A self-adhesive disc on the back enables Sticky Lamp to be fixed to a wall, ceiling or piece of furniture, and a switch located on the power cord turns the light on or off.

Kabel created Sticky Lamp shortly after graduating from Design Academy Eindhoven, and it was promptly put into production by Dutch design label Droog. The shell is manufactured from inexpensive, robust and recyclable PET plastic (commonly used to make bottles and food containers), giving it the look and feel of a disposable object. However, the lamp's playful form – which mimics the outline of the bulb – and the interactive process of sticking the lamp to the wall make it much more personable and less likely to be thrown away.

Product
Styrene

Designer
Paul Cocksedge

Manufacturer
**Paul Cocksedge
Studio**

Date
2003

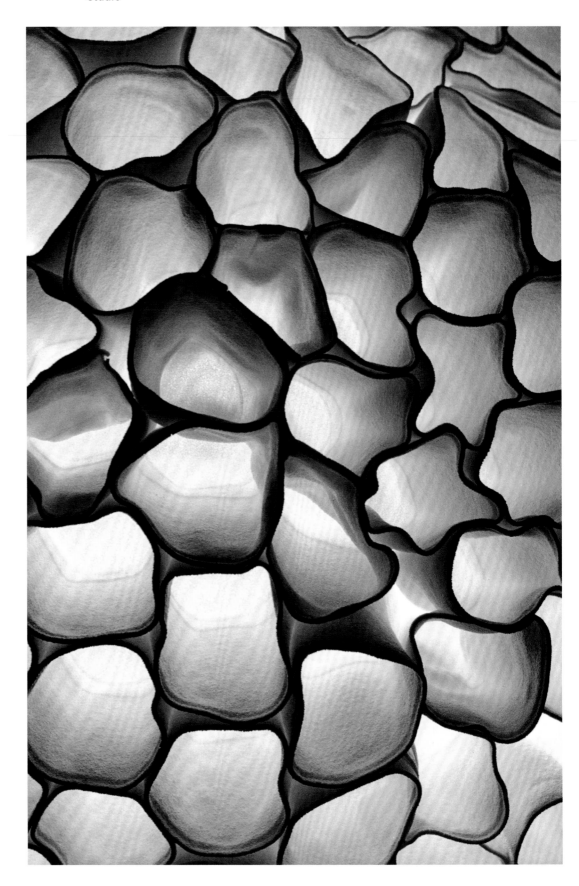

⌐ Melted polystyrene
cups form a rigid cellular
structure that surrounds
the light source.

‹ The uniform mass
produced objects
transform into uniquely
organic forms when heated.

London designer Paul Cocksedge is renowned for his experimental creative process and ability to identify surprising applications for existing or emerging materials and technologies. His designs regularly harness the familiar and emotive properties of light to highlight formal or technical innovations.

Styrene is one of several lighting projects developed by Cocksedge during his studies at the Royal College of Art. Ron Arad, Cocksedge's tutor, introduced him to several influential designers, including Ingo Maurer, who invited him to exhibit Styrene and other pieces at a satellite show during the Milan Furniture Fair in 2003. The product's innovative construction resulted from Cocksedge's fascination with the way polystyrene cups react to heat – transforming from identical mass-produced objects into unique sculptural forms with combined structural strength. Cocksedge developed a technique for melting multiple cups together to create a cellular surface that resembles natural structures such as honeycomb. When illuminated from within, the spherical shade emits a diffused light punctuated by a random pattern created by the rims of the melted cups.

Product	Designer	Manufacturer	Date
Glo-Ball	**Jasper Morrison**	**Flos**	**1999**

∟ Glo-Ball transforms the traditional opal glass shade into a contemporary icon.

❯ Acid etching produces a matt surface that eliminates reflections and creates a warm, even glow.

This seminal product by British designer Jasper Morrison reinvents the traditional opal glass diffuser – synonymous with early twentieth century designs, such as Wilhelm Wagenfeld's Bauhaus table lamp of 1924 – as a pure contemporary form that is extremely versatile. The Glo-Ball family, which consists of a pendant shade and floor and table versions with minimal white powdered stainless steel bases, has proven immensely popular, thanks to its understated yet elegant appearance.

A warm glow emanates from the entire surface of the flashed glass shade, which is made by dipping a bubble of clear glass into molten opal glass before blowing it into the slightly squashed oval form. The completely matt surface is achieved by acid etching the glass. This process adds texture that helps to diffuse the light evenly, making it seem as if the globe itself is illuminated rather than just the bulb. Glo-Ball is typical of Morrison's ability to combine beauty with practicality and create products that become future archetypes.

Product
Light Tray

Designer
**Andreas Engesvik
and Daniel Rybakken**

Manufacturer
Asplund

Date
2011

L Light Tray allows the
user to rearrange glass
domes of varying heights,
diameters and colours to
create different effects.

❯ Muted tones ensure
the hand-blown shades
complement one another,
no matter how they are
combined.

Light Tray is the result of a collaboration between Norwegian designers Andreas Engesvik and Daniel Rybakken, who wanted to challenge traditional lighting typologies and create a product combining illumination with tactility and a sense of mystery.

The user is encouraged to interact with the lamp by reconfiguring the glass domes that shield the bulbs, thereby altering the colour and intensity of the light. A white powder-coated aluminium surface provides a neutral background for the tinted hand-blown domes, which create overlapping areas of differing hues depending on how they are combined. The slightly elevated base seems to float above the surface on which it rests and electrical components and power cables are hidden underneath, giving the impression that the light sources are self-powered. Light Tray was first shown at Spazio Rossana Orlandi in Milan in 2011 and was subsequently put into production by Swedish brand Asplund.

Product
28 series

Designer
Omer Arbel

Manufacturer
Bocci

Date
2009

< Each unique element
is made using traditional
glass blowing techniques
to a formula that allows
for variation.

^ The pendants can be
suspended individually or in
clusters of different colours.

Rather than designing identical products with a rigidly
determined form, Omer Arbel of Vancouver-based
lighting brand Bocci wanted to celebrate the infinite
variance of mouth-blown glass by producing individual
objects that are united by a common process. Each
unique example of his 28 series pendant is made by
reheating sections of the surface of a clear or coloured
glass sphere so that additional molten glass can be
attached and blown to create an internal void. The
position and depth of these voids varies but every
element features a large inner shape made of opaque
milk glass that houses a low-voltage bulb.
        The pendants are designed to cluster in hexagonal
configurations but can also be arranged as infinitely
customisable chandeliers. Any number of elements can
be suspended at different heights, and a limitless palette
of colours can be specified for the external surface.
The 28 series offers a highly customisable alternative
to traditional chandeliers, based on a production
system that supports traditional craft techniques.

Product	Designer	Manufacturer	Date
Lighthouse	**Ronan and Erwan Bouroullec**	**Established & Sons**	**2010**

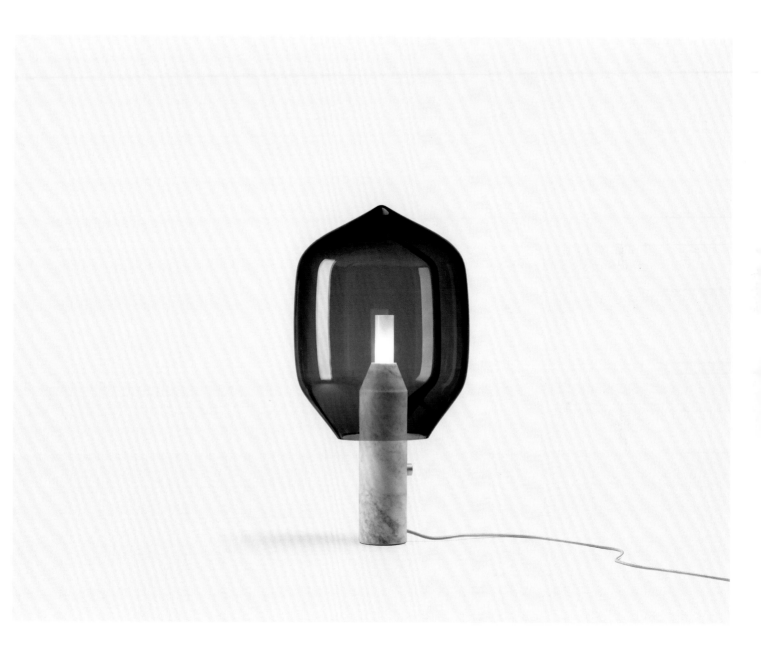

⌐ The voluminous glass shade is balanced on an aluminium support to highlight its fragility.

∧ The design carefully balances handcrafted and machined materials.

As part of a collaboration between British design brand Established & Sons and the legendary Italian glassblowing company Venini, Ronan and Erwan Bouroullec were inspired to design a lamp to celebrate the flawless lucidity of glass. The mouth-blown shade expands outwards from a flattened base, transitioning into an elongated midsection before accumulating at a conical peak. The glass is coloured in traditional shades, and its delicate translucency contrasts with a base of solid white Carrara marble or black Belgian marble. The shade hangs from an aluminium arm, emulating molten glass suspended from the tip of the glassblower's pipe and emphasising the fragility of the material.

The gentle geometric shapes of the base and shade are typical of the French brothers' refined aesthetic style. The product demonstrates how industrial techniques – such as those used to produce the base and arm – can combine with traditional blown glass. The elegant forms focus attention on the precision and quality of finish that can be achieved using each of these methods.

Product
NeON

Designer
Paul Cocksedge

Date
2003

‹ Handmade glass vessels
contain an almost colourless
gas that glows red when a
current is introduced.

˻ The bulbous forms are
aesthetically distinct from
typical neon lighting.

Neon lighting is typically associated with gaudy advertising signage; however, Paul Cocksedge's experimental design diverges from the usual applications and aesthetics, and instead focuses on neon's physical properties. The handmade glass vessels are quite unlike the thin tubes used in most neon lighting: at first glance the cluster of elegantly tapering forms appear to be empty, but when an electric charge is introduced the natural gas inside them produces a warm glow. This surprising transformation is characteristic of Cocksedge's ability to capture the mystery and enchantment of light through the application of scientific techniques. NeON was awarded the Bombay Sapphire Prize for excellence and innovation in contemporary glass design in 2003.

Cocksedge founded his eponymous studio with fellow RCA graduate Joana Pinho in 2004. He has designed lights for companies including Established & Sons and Flos, and produced large-scale artworks including a window display for The Wellcome Trust in London which employed a network of neon tubes to trace the outline of veins and arteries in two enormous arms.

Product	Designer	Manufacturer	Date
Diamonds are a girl's best friend	**Matali Crasset**	**Meta**	**2008**

< The frame of this lantern is made from an ancient Chinese alloy called Paktong.

⌐ A Paktong chain with a unique repeating master link design supports the lantern's weight.

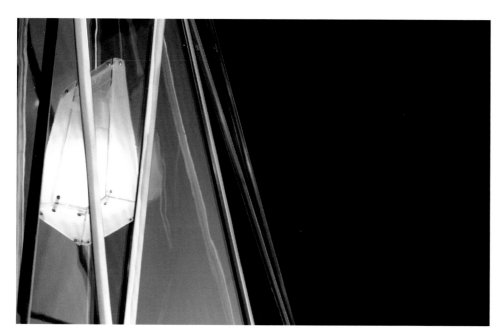

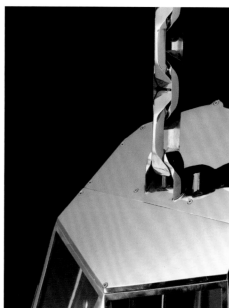

Paktong, an ancient alloy that was imported to England from China in the eighteenth century but that fell out of use during the nineteenth century, was revived by French designer Matali Crasset to produce the faceted frame of this luxurious lantern. Crasset worked with materials scientists at Oxford University and a traditional metal alloy foundry to identify the formula required to reproduce Paktong – a compound of copper, nickel and zinc, which resembles silver and is extremely robust and slow to tarnish. The metal is expertly cast using a lost wax process to create the frame's 102 individual angles, which contain 24 blown-glass panels produced by a specialist sheet glass manufacturer in Germany.

The piece was commissioned by Meta – a company established by the antique dealership Mallett – for its launch collection of artisan-made contemporary products. Leading designers were invited to collaborate with master craftsmen to create products that can only be made in very limited numbers due to the rare materials and complex processes involved in their manufacture.

Product	Designer	Manufacturer	Date
Copper Shade	**Tom Dixon**	**Tom Dixon**	**2005**

L Copper Shade is made using a vacuum metallisation process that applies a microscopically thin layer of copper to the internal surface of a polycarbonate sphere.

› The shades can be used individually or in clusters that produce kaleidoscopic reflections.

Tom Dixon is one of the world's most respected and influential designers of lighting products, and the Copper Shade is among his most iconic creations. The product evolved from a process developed for an earlier design called Mirror Ball, which launched in 2003. This innovative vacuum metallisation technique involves exploding a tiny amount of metal within a vacuum, which bonds itself to the surface of the polycarbonate globe. Copper Shade uses the same process to produce a flawless reflective surface with a warm tone which has made it a popular choice for interior designers seeking a simple statement light that can be used individually or in clusters.

Dixon's furniture and lighting designs are characterised by a materials-led approach that drives him to explore unusual manufacturing techniques and uncover new applications for existing and emerging industrial processes. Having established his reputation in the mid-1980s with a series of welded furniture designs, he continues to develop and self-produce outstanding products and was awarded the OBE for services to British design in 2000.

Product	Designer	Manufacturer	Date
Fold	**Alexander Taylor**	**Established & Sons**	**2005**

‹ A simple net shape is folded to create a self-supporting form that resembles an archetypal lamp.

⌐ The smallest version of Fold is produced from a single sheet of precision cut and bent steel.

Fold is the result of British designer Alexander Taylor's self-initiated quest to design a lamp that uses as few materials as possible and requires a minimum number of processes. Taylor experimented with cut-and-fold paper models to find a way to produce a base and stand with the required stability from a single sheet of material. Having settled on a net shape, he explored materials that would be suitable for mass production, starting with Perspex, then brass, aluminium and finally steel, which offered the necessary rigidity and could be folded without compromising the material's strength. The net shape is laser cut from a steel sheet before being formed on an industrial press.

The product's shape evokes the familiar outline of an archetypal lamp and a classic braided fabric cable adds another nod to tradition, offering a quirky contrast to the modern materials and manufacturing methods. Fold was part of British brand Established & Sons' launch collection and is produced in two table versions and as a larger floor standing lamp.

Product	Designer	Manufacturer	Date
Beat	**Tom Dixon**	**Tom Dixon**	**2006**

∧ The spun brass shapes are inspired by traditional pots and vessels.

˩ Skilled craftsmen in northern India produce the hand beaten finish that gives the internal surface its dimpled texture.

In the pursuit of creating beautiful lighting products, Tom Dixon's work explores innovative contemporary manufacturing methods, as well as engaging with more traditional skills and techniques. The Beat collection is produced using a combination of industrial and craft processes, and its forms are inspired by traditional brass cooking pots and water vessels from the Indian subcontinent.

A sheet of brass is spun and pressed into shape using an industrial tool before the hand-beaten decoration is applied by skilled craftsmen from the city of Moradabad in northern India. Dixon came across these uniquely talented experts in brass while on a visit to Jaipur with his students from the Royal College of Art and developed Beat as a way to give these traditional techniques a contemporary purpose.

Beat is produced in four variations, including a tall, slender cone and a stout, convex bulb shape. The exterior of each lamp is finished in a smooth black or white lacquer, while the internal surface radiates a warm, diffused light that highlights the concentric rings of indentations created by accurate blows from a small hammer.

‹ Heavy Light demonstrates an alternative use for a material more typically associated with the construction industry.

⌐ The raw surface highlights the textural details resulting from the process of pouring and setting the concrete.

A trip to a German workshop that specialises in concrete accessories prompted London designer Benjamin Hubert to explore the possibility of producing an attractive concrete lamp. Hubert was keen to alter the perception of the material by demonstrating that it could be used to make refined and delicate forms that would be suitable for lighting.

The thin-walled shade is made by casting a pure Portland stone aggregate mix in a silicone-based mould. Adding a light source enhances the textural imperfections that result from air bubbles rising to the surface as the poured concrete dries. The surprising application of a familiar material and its raw, untreated finish are typical of Hubert's focus on expressing the inherent personality of materials. Hubert graduated from the Industrial Design and Technology course at Loughborough University before launching his eponymous design studio in 2009. He has designed products for many of the world's most prestigious manufacturers, including Cappellini, Ligne Roset and Poltrona Frau.

Product
**Brave New
World Lamp**

Designer
Freshwest

Manufacturer
Moooi

Date
2008

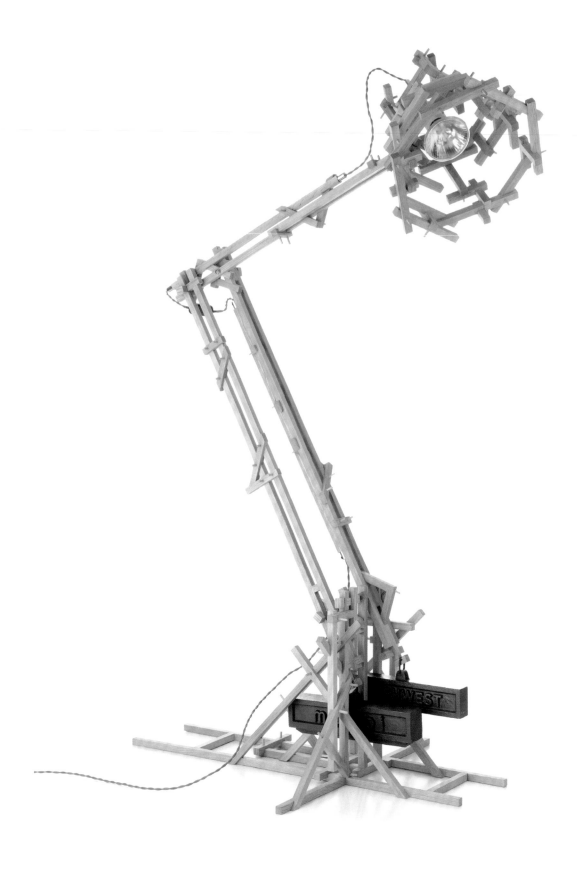

‹ Dozens of small pieces
of solid oak create the
seemingly haphazard
form of the giant Brave
New World Lamp.

⌐ The lamp is produced
in two variations that reach
heights of 180cm and
270cm when fully extended.

Inspired by the aesthetic of bamboo scaffolding,
designers Marcus Beck and Simon Macro set about
creating self-supporting structures with no
predetermined form from small pieces of wood.
They initially built towers that provided support for
a table top but were intent on showing off more of
the structure and so began creating an oversized
articulated light. The lamp's freeform structure is
carefully assembled from pieces of timber that are
notched and pegged together, with cast iron weights
acting as a counterbalance. An initial prototype was
shown during the London Design Festival in 2008
and put into production by Dutch company Moooi,
who manufacture the product in two sizes.

Beck and Macro are childhood friends from
Pembrokeshire, Wales, who both studied fine art
(Beck at Manchester Metropolitan University and
Macro at the University of Brighton) before returning
to Wales and founding Freshwest in 2006. Their
self-initiated designs are represented by several
contemporary galleries, and they also work on
furniture, interiors and branding projects for
commercial clients.

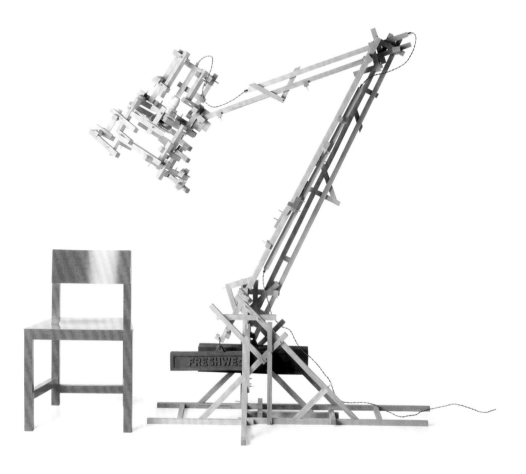

Product
w084t2

Designer
Ilse Crawford

Manufacturer
Wästberg

Date
2008

◄ Contrasting materials enhance the awkward juxtaposition of parts that make articulated lamps so distinctive.

⌐ A cast iron base provides weight and stability, while the translucent plastic shade emits a warm glow.

The use of authentic and untreated materials lends this task light a simplicity and tactility that typifies the human-centred approach of its designer, Ilse Crawford, and her London practice Studioilse. The individual components – a cast iron base for weight, a solid beech arm and a semi-opaque plastic shade – are deliberately kept distinct from one another so their separate functions are clearly expressed. A visible split line between the two sections that form the base hints at the presence of a rotation mechanism, which enables the upper section to swivel. A protruding plastic dial allows the light level to be easily and accurately dimmed.

Crawford is the former founding editor of interiors publication, Elle Decoration UK, and a respected proponent of intelligent and emotional design. Her work focuses on improving everyday experiences by imbuing products and interiors with a sense of warmth and familiarity. In the case of this product, contrasting materials highlight the inherent awkwardness of the articulated form, which is treated as a quality to be celebrated rather than rectified.

Product	Designer	Manufacturer	Date
Wood Lamp	**TAF/Gabriella Gustafson & Mattias Ståhlbom**	**Muuto**	**2008**

∧ Wood Lamp is made from pieces of pine held together by industrial wing nuts.

The wooden workplace is a part of TAF's most recent project for RH Chairs, a conceptual arena to exhibit their furniture.

^ The product was designed as a pragmatic and personable alternative to high-tech desk lamps.

Stockholm-based design studio TAF originally conceived the Wood Lamp as part of an exhibition design for Swedish furniture brand RH Chairs. TAF created a scenography resembling an office using simple props made from untreated pinewood that contrasted with the advanced ergonomic design of the chairs. However, the pleasing proportions of the wooden lamp caught the attention of Scandinavian design brand Muuto, who decided to put it into production.

The product's low-tech look is achieved by reducing the constituent parts of a typical task lamp to basic geometric shapes that are produced using traditional carpentry and joinery techniques. Utilitarian wing nuts hold the sections together and enable the position of the light to be adjusted. Special attention is paid to the positioning of the rubber cord so as not to compromise the lamp's clean lines. Intended as an antidote to the high-tech, performance-led aesthetic of many modern desk lamps, the visible components and straightforward application of a single basic material lend the product an affable appeal.

Product
w101

Designer
**Claesson
Koivisto Rune**

Manufacturer
Wästberg

Date
2010

< A shell moulded from sandwiched sheets of paper supports the electronics and LED light source.

The material is fully biodegradable and made from 100% renewable fibres.

Paper is commonly used to produce shades for lighting products, but with the w101 task light Swedish design studio Claesson Koivisto Rune exploited the material's structural strength when folded to support a custom-designed LED light source. The designers had previously collaborated with Swedish forestry company Södra on the development of a children's chair made using DuraPulp, a material that combines wood pulp from the south of Sweden with a renewable starch-based biopolymer. The light employs the same techniques to create a prototype product that is easy to disassemble, energy efficient and made predominantly from a biodegradable material.

Claesson Koivisto Rune was founded in Stockholm in 1995 by Mårten Claesson, Eero Koivisto and Ola Rune and initially focused on architecture, before expanding into interior, exhibition and product design. Their work displays a typically Swedish sensibility, combining a rational and considered approach to form and materials with playful and whimsical detailing. w101 is a characteristically refined and intelligent product that marries purity of form with an efficient and ecological manufacturing process, resulting in a standout example of contemporary sustainable design.

Product
Pleated Lamp

Designer
Inga Sempé

Manufacturer
Cappellini

Date
2002

‹ The pleated form of
Inga Sempé's oversized
lamp resembles a folded
paper sculpture.

⌐ The use of lightweight
fabric gives the lamp a
fragile appearance, despite
its imposing size.

Standing over two metres tall, this huge yet delicate
floor lamp by French designer Inga Sempé is made
from a lightweight polyester fabric more commonly
used as sailcloth. Sempé's intention was to create
an alternative to the typical standing lamp that relies
on a heavy base to support the light fitting and shade.
The fabric is hung from a minimal wire frame, hidden
so that the textile seems to be self-supporting. Four
low-energy bulbs illuminate the entirety of the form
and highlight the pleated surface.

Born in Paris in 1968, Sempé studied at the city's
École Nationale Supérieure de Création Industrielle
(ENSCI) and worked at some of the world's leading
design studios before founding her own practice in
2000. Her work combines a freedom of expression with
an understanding of materials and three dimensionality
that has resulted in a catalogue of products for clients,
including Luceplan, Ligne Roset and Alessi.

Product
Flex Lamp

Designer
**Sam Hecht
and Kim Colin/
Industrial Facility**

Manufacturer
Droog

Date
2003

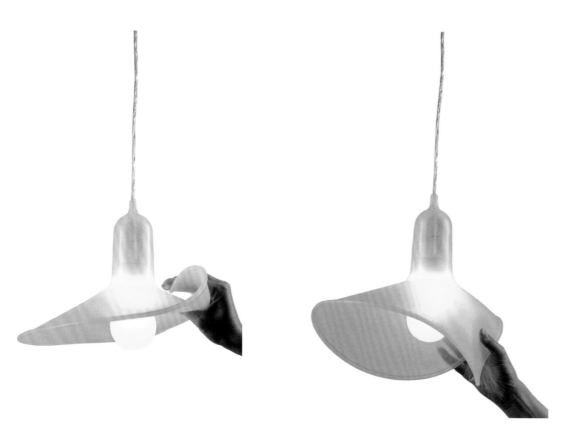

‹ Flex Lamp looks like
a solid pendant shade but
is made from flexible
silicone rubber.

⌐ The rubber acts as a
diffuser, as well as giving
the product a tactile
quality.

This lampshade derives from the designers' desire
to confront the ugliness and harsh light provided by
conventional energy-saving light bulbs. Flex Lamp
treats the bulb like a filament, concealing it within
a silicone rubber skin that lends the light source the
appearance of a traditional incandescent bulb and
creates a softer, diffused light. The bulb cover is designed
to attach simply to the shade, which is moulded from
a single piece of soft rubber. A technically challenging
material development process was required to facilitate
the production of this seamless rubber form with its
well-known silhouette.

Sam Hecht was born in London in 1969 and studied
at Central St Martins before completing a master's at
the Royal College of Art in 1993. He cofounded Industrial
Facility in 2002 with his partner Kim Colin, who obtained
her master's in architecture at SCI-Arc in Los Angeles.
Their work responds to specific cultural and contextual
scenarios with intelligent interventions, executed with
clarity and the needs of the user as the driving factor.

Product
Torch Light

Designer
Sylvain Willenz

Manufacturer
Established & Sons

Date
2008

⌐ Torch Light can be used as a table lamp, as a single suspension light, or clustered in groups of 10 or 20 units to create a chandelier.

‹ The form resembles a robust hand torch but is made from a surprisingly soft and flexible rubber.

References to two iconic objects give Sylvain Willenz's Torch Light a familiar appearance. The graphic silhouette of the lamp's body draws inspiration from the shape of a hand torch, while the diffuser, made from diamond-textured clear polycarbonate, emulates the effect of light refracting from a car headlight and creates a soft, glare-free glow. The lamp's body is made from a flexible PVC-dipped polymer with a matt texture redolent of the tactile handle of a torch.

Differently shaped and sized variations and the option to specify contrasting shade and cable colours add to the product's versatility and have helped it become one of the most popular designs produced by British label Established & Sons. Belgian designer Willenz's work combines an exploratory approach to form and materials with an uncomplicated aesthetic sensibility, evident in Torch Light's playful and accessible design.

Product
Hope

Designer
**Francisco Gomez
Paz and Paolo
Rizzatto**

Manufacturer
Luceplan

Date
2009

An array of polycarbonate lenses replicates the effect of a traditional crystal chandelier.

The use of lightweight contemporary materials makes the product easy to transport and assemble.

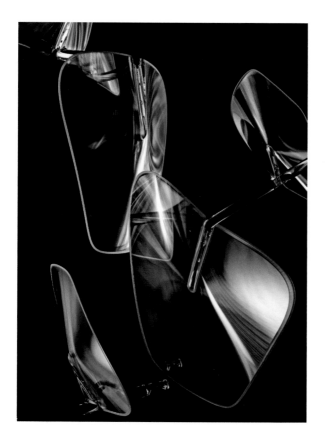

This chandelier is named after the legendary Hope Diamond and attempts to emulate its glittering appearance by employing a series of extremely thin and lightweight polycarbonate lenses to fragment and disperse light. Developed by Italian designer Paolo Rizzatto and Argentinian Francisco Gomez Paz, the product represents a contemporary twist on the idea of the traditional crystal chandelier and consists of transparent 'leaves' imprinted with a series of microprisms, which are based on the Fresnel lenses commonly found in lighthouses and car headlamps. The lenses distort their surroundings and cast dynamic patterns onto the ceiling and walls, while limiting glare from the light source.

The chandelier is assembled by clipping the lenses onto a series of transparent polycarbonate rods, which in turn are fastened to a stainless steel frame. This simple construction and the minimal use of materials make the product extremely light and easy to transport. Hope has been awarded several prizes, including the prestigious Red Dot Design Award in 2010.

Product
Miss K

Designer
Philippe Starck

Manufacturer
Flos

Date
2003

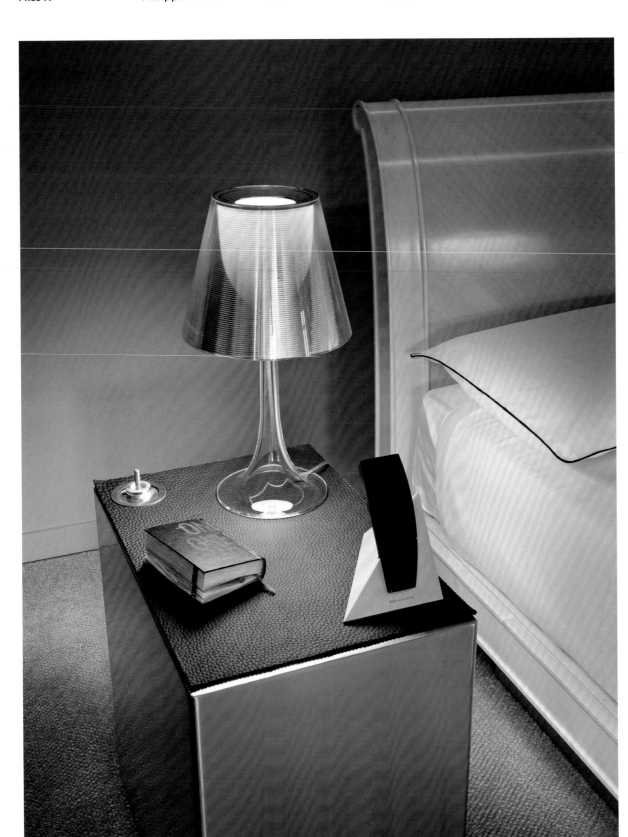

> Miss K is one of
Philippe Starck's most
innovative and popular
lighting designs.

< The metallic
appearance of the shade
gives way to reveal the
internal diffuser when
the light is turned on.

Miss K is one of the most iconic products created by
the world's most famous product designer, Philippe
Starck. Launched a year after his enormously popular
polycarbonate Louis Ghost chair (Kartell, 2002), the
lamp reasserts Starck's mastery of plastic – exploiting
an innovative technology to create a surprising illusion.
The inside of the polycarbonate shade is treated with
a high-vacuum aluminisation process that renders it
metallic. When illuminated, light penetrates the thin
metal layer and reveals the curving form of the inner
diffuser. The lamp's base is made from transparent,
injection-moulded plastic and a dimmer switch on the
cord allows the light output to be accurately adjusted.

As with Louis Ghost, Miss K contrasts an archetypal
form with contemporary materials and manufacturing
processes. The product quickly became a global bestseller
and epitomises Starck's poetic yet practical approach
to rethinking everyday objects. His prolific output
includes several successful lighting designs for Italian
brand Flos, including Miss Sissi (1990), Cicatrices de
Luxe (1998) and Gun Lamp (see pages 058 and 059).
He has also created lights for other companies
including Alessi, Target and Dedon.

Product
Mite and Tite

Designer
Marc Sadler

Manufacturer
Foscarini

Date
2000

< Mite and Tite are made from fibreglass mixed with Kevlar® or carbon thread to give them greater rigidity.

˥ It took Sadler and Foscarini two years to develop a material strong enough to support itself and delicate enough to diffuse light.

Marc Sadler drew upon his experiences designing sports equipment when developing these innovative lightweight lamps. The Milan-based, Austrian-born designer had experimented with composite materials while working on the design of a revolutionary thermoplastic ski boot in the early 1970s and was keen to apply similarly performing materials to realise his vision for a large lamp that is both delicate and robust.

Mite (floor lamp) and Tite (suspension lamp) are made from fibreglass mixed with a yellow Kevlar® or black carbon thread that hardens when baked in a kiln, enabling the elongated forms to hold their shape. The material creates a rigid surface that is thin enough to allow light to penetrate the entire length of the shade, and the high-tech fibres also create a densely banded surface decoration. Mite received the prestigious Compasso D'Oro design award in 2001, and Italian lighting brand Foscarini has since worked with Sadler to apply the innovative process to a range of lighting products.

Product
Hanabi

Designer
Nendo

Date
2006

  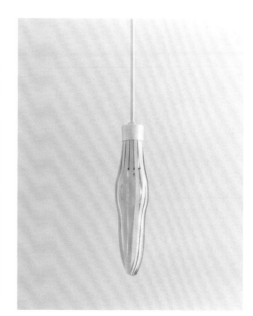

‹   When the light is turned on, heat from the bulb stimulates the surrounding metal strips to fan out.

˥   The lamp is made from a shape-memory alloy that responds to heat by returning to a predetermined position.

This pendant shade by Japanese design studio Nendo is made from strips of metal that undergo a thermomechanical transition when prompted by heat from the light bulb, unfurling like the petals of a flower to reveal the light source. The metal strips are formed from a shape-memory alloy that 'remembers' its original shape and reverts back to this position when heated. No additional mechanisms or electronics are required to induce the peculiar and poetic transformation.

'Hanabi' is the Japanese word for fireworks and translates literally as 'fire flower', a description that perfectly encapsulates the product's appearance and behaviour. The light's simple yet surprising character is typical of Nendo's quest to create products that combine functionality with humour, while retaining an understated Japanese sensibility. Founded by the Canadian-born Japanese designer Oki Sato in 2002, Nendo swiftly established itself as one of Japan's leading design studios, working across many disciplines for clients, including Cappellini, Foscarini, Hermès and Starbucks.

Product	Designer	Manufacturer	Date
Random	**Bertjan Pot**	**Moooi**	**2002**

∟ A delicate skin of hardened glass fibres creates an ethereal and luminous surface.

❯ The light source is fixed to a chromed steel rod that clamps onto the rigid shell.

During his studies at Design Academy Eindhoven, Dutch designer Bertjan Pot explored the technical and sculptural properties of textiles. His 1998 graduation project involved stretching fabric coated in resin around a cluster of balloons to produce a lumpy light shade and proved the starting point for the development of the Random light. It took Pot and the manufacturer, Moooi, three years to translate the experiment into a product, which is made by winding resin-soaked glass fibres around an inflatable spherical mould that can be deflated when the resin has set and removed through a precisely positioned hole in the hardened skin. The dense web of translucent fibres produces a diaphanous surface that transforms into a glowing orb when the bulb is illuminated.

Initially made by hand, production was mechanised as the piece became increasingly popular. Building a machine to perform a task that is 'random' but requires a certain level of control provided a challenge that led to the creation of the Non-Random Light, a spin-off with evenly spaced fibres.

Product	Designer	Manufacturer	Date
Tenda	**Benjamin Hubert**	**Benjamin Hubert Ltd**	**2012**

< Techniques and materials from kite making and sportswear and underwear production are all incorporated into this lightweight design.

⌐ The light is diffused by layers of stretchy fabric suspended from and stretched over a tensile framework.

This series of textile lamps takes its name from the Italian word for 'tent' and draws inspiration from lightweight materials and manufacturing methods. Fibreglass rods used in kite-making, Lycra™ fabric more commonly seen in sportswear and four-way mesh fabric usually used to make underwear all combine to create a diaphanous tensile form.

Brass connectors hold the flexible fibreglass poles in tension, creating a framework within which a suspended layer of Lycra™ acts as a diffuser. The frame is sheathed in a stretchy multidirectional fabric that creates a bulbous form – the opacity of which changes when viewed from different angles. The application of an elastic textile for a lighting product is reminiscent of the iconic tubular Falkland Lamp created by Italian designer Bruno Munari for Danese in 1964; however, the use of cutting-edge fabrics and composite materials brings this process up-to-date. Hubert's studio developed the product entirely in-house to demonstrate that designers don't always need to rely on established manufacturers to bring new products to market.

Product	Designer	Manufacturer	Date
Etch	**Tom Dixon**	**Tom Dixon**	**2010**

L The delicate patterned surface is created by a photo-acid etching technique typically used to make electronic components.

> Light penetrating the perforated metal surface of the Etch light casts intricate shadows on the wall.

Tom Dixon developed the Etch collection using fabrication technologies more commonly associated with the manufacture of circuit boards and other electronic components. A metal sheet just 0.4mm thick is photo etched with an intricate pattern before being exposed to acid that dissolves the weakened metal, leaving behind the delicate filigree. When illuminated, light refracts around the internal surfaces and dissipates through the thousands of tiny holes, casting complex patterns on the wall. The original brass version of Etch was presented at the Milan Furniture Fair in 2010, where staff in a temporary 'factory' assembled the products by folding and fixing them into faceted forms. Stainless steel and copper versions were introduced in 2012, and a smaller candleholder is also available.

The techniques employed in the production of Etch reflect Dixon's interest in streamlining design and manufacturing processes, enabling him to get products to customers faster and stay one step ahead of imitators. The material and pattern could also feasibly be altered quickly, allowing new variations to be regularly introduced.

Product
Fragile Future

Designer
**Lonneke Gordijn
and Ralph Nauta**

Manufacturer
**Carpenters
Workshop Gallery**

Date
2005

‹   Each of the LED
bulbs in this delicate light
sculpture is covered in
dandelion seeds.

⌐   Modules can be
combined from any
direction, creating infinite
possible configurations.

For her graduation project from Design Academy
Eindhoven in 2005, Lonneke Gordijn developed a light
sculpture based on an imagined future in which nature
and technology rely on one another to thrive and evolve.
A maze-like modular circuit of phosphorous bronze
carries power to individual LEDs, each of which is covered
in dandelion seeds that are glued by hand to the surface
of the bulb, recreating a dandelion clock.

   Following her graduation, Gordijn founded a studio
in Amsterdam with her partner and fellow Design
Academy alumnus Ralph Nauta. Together they refined
the product, adding greater three-dimensionality and
increasing the rigidity of the structure. Each module
contains three LEDs and is laser cut and bent using
fifteen different bending moulds. Initially produced as
a wall-hung artwork, the modules can also be combined
to create specially commissioned installations and
chandeliers, including a variation built around a
concrete core which won the Moët Hennessy design
award in 2010 and has since entered the permanent
collection of London's Victoria and Albert Museum.

Product
Court Circuit

Designer
Matali Crasset

Manufacturer
Danese

Date
2011

∟ Court Circuit is made from the same raw material as the printed circuit boards typically used to carry power to LED light sources.

⌐ The circuits branch out across the surface, duplicating and decreasing in thickness like the veins on a leaf.

Court Circuit deliberately exposes technology that is essential to all LED products but is usually hidden from view. The five 'petals' that form the pendant shade are made from the same glass-reinforced epoxy sheets used to manufacture printed circuit boards, and the wires that carry the current to 90 LEDs distributed across the surfaces become a decorative detail.

The product is intended to bring a sense of familiarity to a technology that is still novel and achieves this by referencing nature in the shape of the shade and the branching route of the circuits. These veined lines become more visible as light glows through the 2mm thick semi-opalline surfaces.

The LEDs are carefully arranged to distribute an even downward light, while three bulbs on the outside of each petal and small holes punched in the surfaces emit an ambient glow. As well as alluding to nature, the form also references archetypal lampshades, resulting in a product that is both technologically progressive and reassuringly recognisable.

Product
Hexalights

Designer
Marcus Tremonto

Manufacturer
Treluce Studios

Date
2011

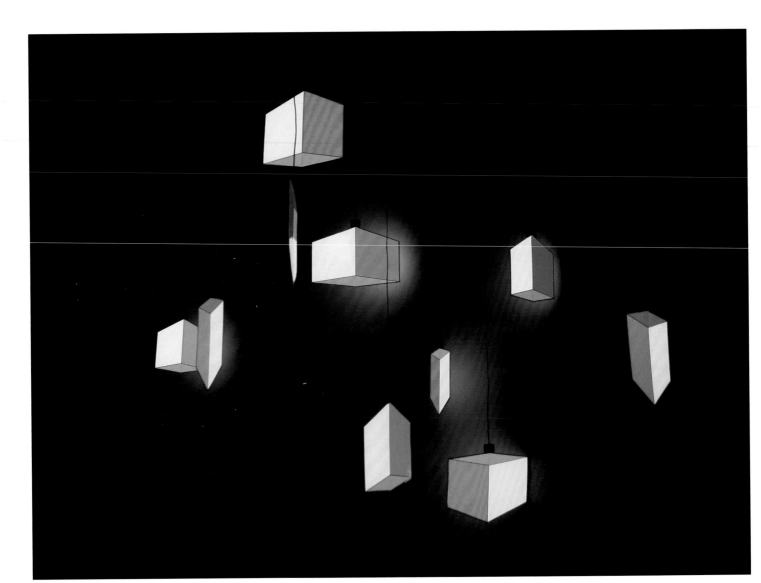

∧ Hexalights resemble
a cartoon cube seen from
different angles.

˥ The lights are made
from a flat sheet of
electroluminescent material
that emits light evenly
across its surface.

These cartoon-like lights give the illusion of three-dimensional form but are, in fact, made from a sheet of electroluminescent material just 1.5mm thick. Drawing inspiration from architecture as well as illustrations seen in 1960s French comics, the design mimics the outline of a hexahedron cube viewed from different perspectives. The lights' true dimensionality becomes apparent as the user moves around them. Newly developed printing techniques were used to enable pop-art colours to be transferred onto the surface of the electroluminescent film.

American-born Marcus Tremonto studied mathematics and physics before completing a master's in fine art at the Art Institute of Chicago. His work expresses a desire to stimulate curiosity through the application of science, technology and visual trickery. He founded Treluce Studios in 2002 with his wife, Monica Tremonto, and has exhibited internationally, including as part of the Swarovski Crystal Palace presentation at the Milan Furniture Fair in 2008. Hexalights evolved from an earlier series of 2D electroluminescent sculptures designed for New York's Moss gallery in 2010.

Technology

< Wallpiercing

The futuristic appearance
and functional versatility
of Ron Gilad's Wallpiercing
demonstrates that lighting
design is entering exciting
and unfamiliar territory.

Throughout the twentieth century the physical dimensions and luminescent properties of the ubiquitous incandescent light bulb informed the appearance and performance of the majority of lighting products. Alternatives, including halogen lamps and fluorescent tubes, found limited applications in commercial and domestic environments, but were never truly embraced by consumers. The gradual phasing out of incandescent bulbs in the twenty-first century has prompted manufacturers to focus on developing more efficient alternatives. Their determination to promote these new products has provoked a frenzy of creative activity and a critical re-examination of lighting's role in domestic, commercial, artistic and architectural scenarios. This section examines alternatives to incandescent lighting through innovative projects that exploit the reduced dimensions, increased efficiency and functional flexibility that these technologies provide.

As the sale of incandescent light bulbs is steadily outlawed around the world, the compact fluorescent lamp (CFL) currently offers the most technologically mature and affordable alternative. CFLs have similar dimensions to traditional tungsten-filament bulbs and produce an equivalent light output but with greatly reduced energy consumption. They evolved from the familiar fluorescent tubes first developed for commercial use in the early twentieth century, which achieved widespread popularity in offices and institutional environments. The earliest coiled compact version was invented by Edward Hammer, an engineer at General Electric, in 1976. It was subsequently copied and refined by other manufacturers – eventually becoming more efficient and affordable. However, the CFL has become notorious for its cold, unattractive light and clumsy appearance, which lacks the elegance of its predecessor. With its market dominance increasing, several attempts at improving the CFL have begun to emerge, including the Plumen 001 by British product design company Hulger and designer Samuel Wilkinson. Their bulb reconfigures the tubes as sinuous, intertwining lines and uses better quality components that help to produce a light with a warmer colour temperature than typical CFLs. The widespread adoption of the CFL can be attributed to its relative affordability in comparison to other alternative light sources; however, it offers little scope for continued development and is already being usurped by emerging technologies with enhanced performance and functionality.

Of the alternative lighting technologies that have made it to market, light-emitting diodes (LEDs) have made the most significant impact on lighting design in recent years. These light sources are made from an inorganic semiconductor material that releases energy as light when exposed to a current. LEDs were initially used as indicator lights and displays in electronic equipment, but the evolution of brighter versions has seen the number of potential applications increase incrementally. LEDs offer several advantages over more conventional light sources: they can be extremely small (less than 1mm²) and are generally powered by a low voltage current so they don't require the same bulky fittings as incandescent and fluorescent bulbs. They can be arranged on surfaces to disperse a diffused light or

clustered together to replicate a point light source. Linking red, green and blue LEDs to electronic circuits that control the individual bulbs offers the possibility to create a full spectrum of coloured light that can be adjusted dynamically.

Currently, the most common domestic application for LEDs is in task lighting. Groups of LEDs provide sufficient close-range illumination to make them particularly suitable for use in work spaces. The slimline form of Antonio Citterio and Toan Nguyen's Kelvin LED desk light celebrates the minimal dimensions of the light source, while Jake Dyson's technical CSYS task light uses a copper pipe to draw heat away from the LEDs, helping them achieve a life span of at least 160,000 hours. German lighting legend Ingo Maurer was the first designer to develop lamps using LEDs for residential use. His experimental projects – including a wallpaper with a repeat pattern comprising hundreds of functioning LEDs – are helping to initiate a re-evaluation of interior lighting based on the radically different physical properties of this evolving technology.

Several technologies currently being developed have the potential to transform the way light sources are used in products and interiors. Electroluminescent materials that emit light when exposed to a current can be used to create wafer-thin luminous surfaces. Organic light-emitting diodes (OLEDs) are made from a semiconductor material consisting of organic compounds and are currently being used in screens and digital displays, as they offer excellent efficiency and high resolution. Electronics companies, including Philips and German firm Novaled AG, manufacture OLED light sources as flat panels that emit an even light across their entire surface. The first commercially available OLED light source was the Lumiblade panel, launched by Philips in 2009. Since then, Philips has engaged several leading designers, including Amanda Levete and rAndom International, to develop innovative products and installations that utilise the Lumiblade technology. These projects exploit the thinness and homogeneous light quality achieved by OLEDs, but their light output and cost need to be addressed before they can hope to achieve significant market penetration. As with all emerging technologies, there is uncertainty about the most suitable applications for OLEDs, and a period of refinement and reflection is required before their true benefits become clear.

New technologies that are too expensive to be mass-produced often find their earliest applications in artistic projects. Lighting technologies hold particular appeal because light itself is naturally expressive and offers a familiar base upon which to build new experiences. Several festivals dedicated to lighting in the urban environment have been inaugurated in recent years, including Lumiere in Durham, England, which first illuminated the medieval city's buildings, streets and bridges in 2009. For the 2011 edition of the annual Festival of Lights in Lyon, France, British designer Paul Cocksedge created a magical installation using electroluminescent sheets that seemed to be blowing across a seventeenth century courtyard in the heart of the city. The innovative properties of contemporary light sources, such as LEDs and electroluminescent

‹ Showtime
Architectural installations,
such as Showtime by
Jason Bruges Studio,
utilise digital control
systems to programme
the behaviour of lighting
on a spectacular scale.

materials, offer unusual effects that add to the technical spectacle of these temporary, site-specific interventions.

Lighting has become a popular medium for a new generation of creatives working in digital design, as advances in computer software and digital control systems enable the behaviour of light sources to be managed and customised. The work of designers such as Troika, rAndom International, UVA and Jason Bruges Studio uses interactive technologies to re-examine the relationships between people and objects. Sensor-based systems facilitate the development of immersive experiences that respond to stimuli such as sound or movement. The results can be surprisingly poetic, such as Simon Heijdens' projection of a tree that sheds a leaf when someone walks by it. Sonumbra, by Loop.pH, invites people to shelter beneath the glowing surface of a lace-like parasol displaying patterns of light that gravitate towards them, while UVA's Volume installation consists of LED-covered, sound-emitting columns that react to the presence of people by producing a shifting audio-visual environment. These installations invite participation and use light to provide visual feedback when provoked by human interaction.

In addition to sensors that detect tangible stimuli, contemporary light sources can also combine with systems linked to cameras or digital communication technologies, such as SMS messages or RSS feeds. The data these sources gather is converted into visualisations, which are then displayed using customised lighting. Pixel Cloud by Jason Bruges Studio, for example, collects information about the local weather from cameras on the roof of a building in London and translates this into a live simulation that plays out across a matrix of coloured LED spheres suspended in the atrium below. German studio KRAM/WEISSHAAR programmed robots from a car assembly plant to create light paintings based on messages uploaded onto a custom-built website. In the domestic environment, similar technologies are already being used in integrated systems that allow homeowners to control lighting using touch panels, remote controls or applications downloaded onto a phone or mobile device. These systems could soon enable light to respond intuitively to the user's presence and actions – and perhaps even mood – by automatically adjusting their position, intensity and colour. This logical progression will lead to more intuitive but less tangible interaction with lighting in the home.

The potential for programming the behaviour of light sources is also being applied on a much larger scale, with the development of illuminated installations that turn the surfaces of entire buildings into dynamic artworks or giant billboards. These media façades generally offer a low-resolution display, suitable for rendering abstract graphics and patterns rather than high-quality images or video. A pioneering example is the BIX installation, designed by multidisciplinary studio realities:united in 2003 for the façade of the Kunsthaus Graz art gallery in Austria. An array of fluorescent tubes fitted behind the building's undulating Plexiglass skin displays specially commissioned low-resolution monochrome animations that can be seen by the public from the nearby riverbank. Similar to its

reactive Pixel Cloud installation, Jason Bruges Studio's exterior illumination for the W Hotel in London's Leicester Square is based on images of the surrounding skyline taken by cameras on the hotel's roof throughout the day. The pictures are then compiled to create an abstract animated pattern that is displayed on the façade after dark by several hundred LED light tubes. These projects provide a dynamic and performative public presence that exploits the attention-grabbing quality of light to transform buildings into beacons within dense urban environments.

Whether applied to large-scale interventions, temporary installations or more ecological domestic lighting, the key benefits of advanced lighting technologies are improved efficiency and greater levels of control and customisability. The enforced introduction of efficient alternatives to incandescent bulbs has sparked an ongoing process of research and development that consistently yields impressive and potentially revolutionary results. For designers, the reduced dimensions, colour-rendering properties and interactive potential of these new technologies enable light to be treated as a responsive and adaptable material. The appearance of light sources may have changed forever, but our emotional connection to light remains the same and will always inform future generations of lighting. Above all, new light sources and lighting products should prioritise the quality of light and experience, regardless of the technology used.

Product	Designer	Manufacturer	Date
Plumen 001	**Hulger and Samuel Wilkinson**	**Hulger**	**2010**

> ❯ Plumen 001 was designed as an alternative to ugly energy-saving light bulbs.

> ❮ From one angle, the intertwining tubes form the outline of a traditional incandescent bulb.

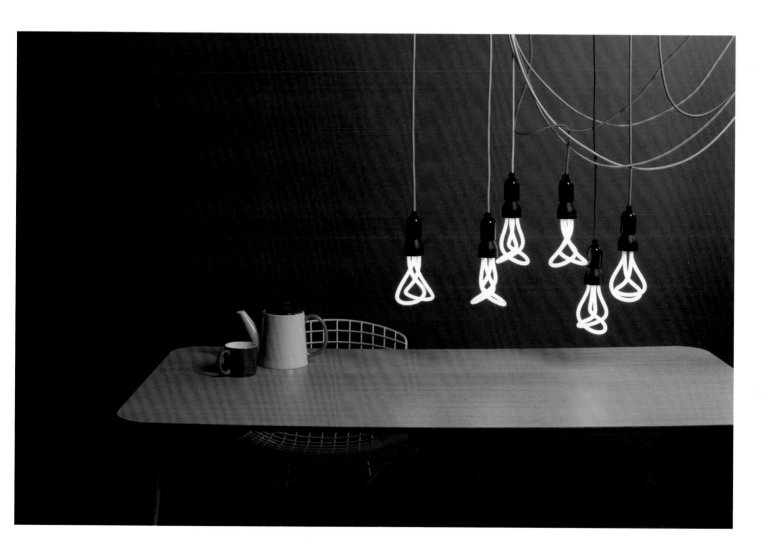

Plumen 001 was developed by British lighting brand
Hulger in response to what it perceived as the lack
of an attractive alternative to low-energy light bulbs.
Hulger and British designer Samuel Wilkinson
examined the manufacturing processes used to
produce compact fluorescent lamps and identified
areas where aesthetic and technical improvements
could be made. Most importantly, they endeavoured
to create a form that was attractive enough to stand
on its own as a sculptural presence in a room.

The bulb reinterprets the twisting, gas-filled tubes
of typical CFLs as a dynamic arrangement of two
symmetrical pieces. The unique and distinctive form
adds value, allowing better quality components and
materials to be specified. This results in a bulb that
illuminates faster and has a warmer colour temperature
than standard CFLs. London's Design Museum awarded
Plumen 001 its Design of the Year prize in 2011, and the
bulb has been inducted into the permanent collections
of several of the world's top design museums.

Product
EL.E.Dee

Designer
Ingo Maurer

Manufacturer
Ingo Maurer GmbH

Date
2001

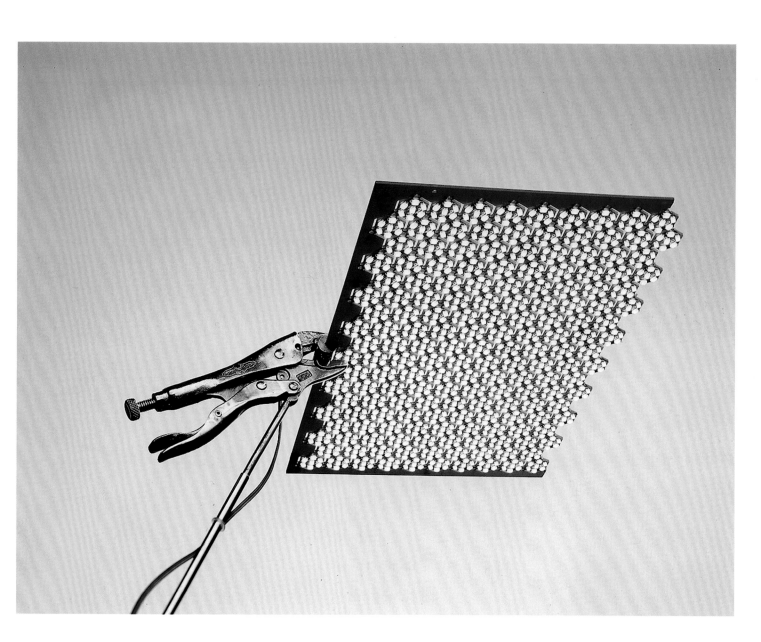

⌐ Products such as
EL.E.Dee pioneered the use
of emerging LED technology
in domestic lighting.

∧ An LED-covered circuit
board is attached to the
stem with a small pair of
wrench pliers.

Visionary German lighting designer Ingo Maurer
created the first residential lamp incorporating
LED light sources in 1997. Called Bellissima Brutta,
the lamp's base is made from a cube of printed
circuit boards from which wires supporting round
LED-covered panels sprout like a bunch of flowers.
Maurer's ongoing experimentation with LEDs resulted
in several epochal products that deliberately exposed
the workings of this unfamiliar light source.

One of Maurer's most iconic LED creations, EL.E.Dee
is an interpretation of an adjustable lamp that has been
stripped back to its basic components. The light source
is clamped to a simple stem with a small pair of vice
wrench pliers, as if it has just been fabricated in the
workshop. A ball-and-socket joint connects the stem
to the base, allowing the direction of the light to be
adjusted. The bulbs and circuitry of the LED panel
are left uncovered, celebrating the intrinsic beauty
of the technology.

Product	Designer	Manufacturer	Date
Kelvin LED	**Antonio Citterio and Toan Nguyen**	**Flos**	**2009**

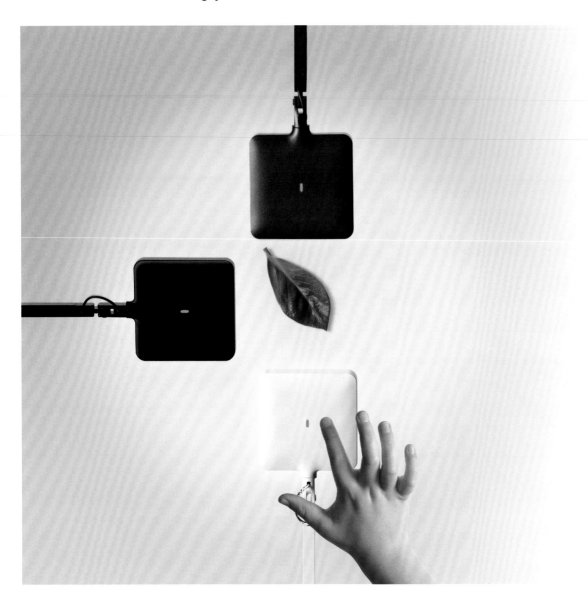

❮ Kelvin LED combines new technologies with a familiar and intuitive form.

⌐ A pantograph mechanism enables easy adjustment of the extruded aluminium arm.

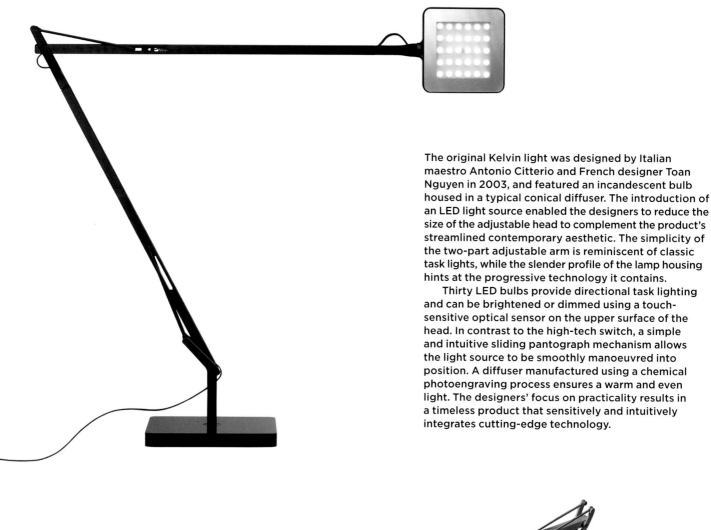

The original Kelvin light was designed by Italian maestro Antonio Citterio and French designer Toan Nguyen in 2003, and featured an incandescent bulb housed in a typical conical diffuser. The introduction of an LED light source enabled the designers to reduce the size of the adjustable head to complement the product's streamlined contemporary aesthetic. The simplicity of the two-part adjustable arm is reminiscent of classic task lights, while the slender profile of the lamp housing hints at the progressive technology it contains.

Thirty LED bulbs provide directional task lighting and can be brightened or dimmed using a touch-sensitive optical sensor on the upper surface of the head. In contrast to the high-tech switch, a simple and intuitive sliding pantograph mechanism allows the light source to be smoothly manoeuvred into position. A diffuser manufactured using a chemical photoengraving process ensures a warm and even light. The designers' focus on practicality results in a timeless product that sensitively and intuitively integrates cutting-edge technology.

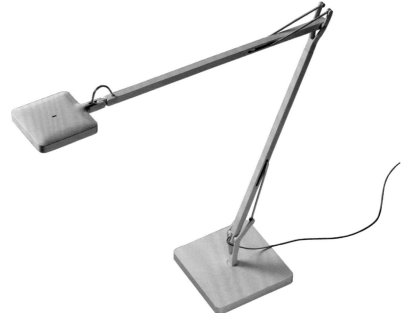

Product
CSYS

Designer
Jake Dyson

Manufacturer
Jake Dyson Studio

Date
2011

‹ The CSYS task light features a bearing-based mechanism for easy and accurate positioning.

⌄ A copper pipe draws heat away from the light source, removing the need for additional pumps or energy to cool the LEDs.

HEAT IN

HEAT OUT

HEAT IN

HEAT OUT

New technologies and innovative engineering principles converge in the design of the CSYS task light by British designer Jake Dyson. Dissatisfied with the maneuverability of existing desk lamps, Dyson took inspiration from construction cranes and drawing boards and created a bearing-based mechanism that allows the position of the light source to be smoothly adjusted through three axes. This enables the light to be directed as a brightly focused spot or a larger pool, depending on the task being performed. The mechanism also holds the lamp accurately in place once it has been positioned.

The product's other key innovation is the way it manages the thermal output of the LEDs, which greatly affects their longevity. Heat is drawn away from the light source and dissipated along the length of a copper pipe contained within the cantilevered arm. This innovative application of a technology, more commonly found in satellites and computer processors, ensures the light source achieves a life span of at least 160,000 hours.

Product	Designer	Manufacturer	Date
My New Flame	**Moritz Waldemeyer**	**Ingo Maurer GmbH**	**2012**

‹ My New Flame replicates the functionality and appearance of a candle using contemporary technologies.

⌐ The flickering image of a flame is reproduced using a double-sided LED display.

This contemporary reinvention of the candlestick uses sophisticated technology to recreate the image of a flame flickering in the wind. At the upper end of a narrow black circuit board, a double-sided display featuring 128 tiny LEDs on each side is programmed to show the moving image of a flame that will never burn down. LEDs with a warm colour temperature mimic the natural glow of candlelight and achieve a light output roughly equivalent to that of a standard candle.

German designer Moritz Waldemeyer came up with the idea for the poetic combination of light and technology, which was developed with the assistance of Ingo Maurer and his team. Waldemeyer regularly collaborates with architects and fashion designers such as Zaha Hadid, Ron Arad and Hussein Chalayan (see pages 204 and 205) on projects that use technology to introduce unexpected behaviours. His London studio was responsible for translating the image of the flame into pixel data, which was then used by a software engineer to programme the individual LEDs.

Product
Little Sun

Designer
**Olafur Eliasson and
Frederik Ottesen**

Manufacturer
Little Sun GmbH

Date
2012

< The sun-shaped light is fitted with photovoltaic panels that generate and store power during the day to be used at night.

◹ Sales of the light help to make it available at a reduced cost to people living without electricity.

Little Sun is a portable solar-powered light developed by Danish-Icelandic artist Olafur Eliasson and engineer Frederik Ottesen to confront and raise awareness of the plight of the 1.6 billion people worldwide who live without access to mains electricity. The playful and tactile product features a 60mm x 60mm photovoltaic cell on the back that provides light to last an evening when charged in the sun for at least five hours.

The project operates as a social business – the profits generated by sales of the product (in parts of the world with electricity) help to supply the product to small businesses in the developing world at a greatly reduced cost. A launch event at London's Tate Modern gallery in 2012 encouraged visitors to buy a light that they could then use to navigate the collections of Surrealist and Realist art. Little Sun not only functions as a practical tool for those living without electricity, but as an artwork and a means of communicating this critical social issue to a wider public.

Product	Designer	Manufacturer	Date
Raimond	**Raimond Puts**	**Moooi**	**2006**

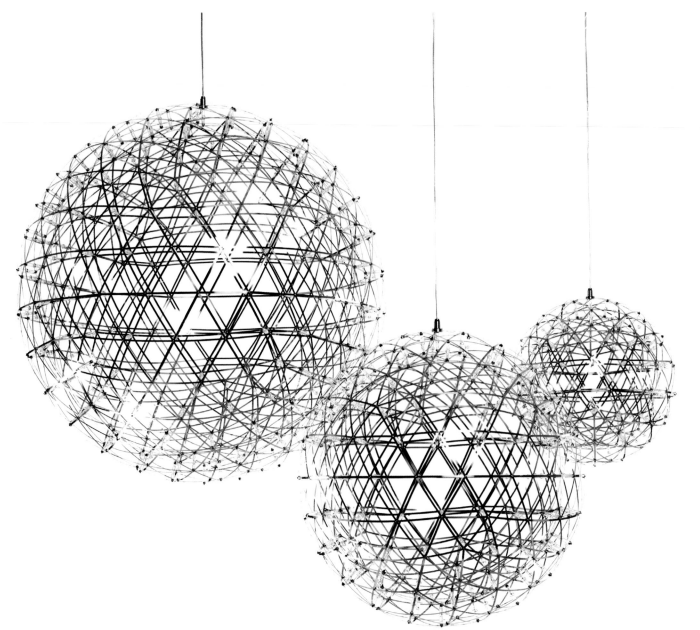

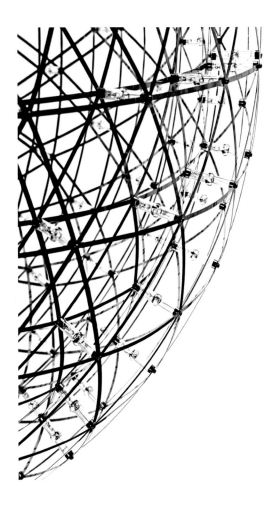

A lifelong fascination with mathematical principles informed the sophisticated geodesic structure of this light fitting by Belgian designer Raimond Puts. Puts studied metalwork and worked as a lathe operator and a social worker, but in his spare time he would regularly build models from low-cost materials, such as paper, iron strips and mosquito nets, to test the functional potential of geometric shapes.

Raimond is inspired by the interlocking cells of a football and is composed of two layers of stainless steel strips that carry a current to dozens of LEDs fixed between the layers. The precise design invokes the geodesic forms developed by pioneering American engineer Richard Buckminster Fuller and lends the product a visual and physical lightness that belies its structural strength. When the LEDs are illuminated, the graphic pattern of the steel matrix gives way to a constellation of individual light points. Puts was in his mid-seventies when the design was put into production by Moooi, allowing him to finally realise the result of decades of research and experimentation.

∧   A double-layered matrix of steel strips carries current to LEDs fixed between them.

‹   The lightweight structure is based on precise mathematical principles.

Product
Thixotropes

Designer
Troika

Date
2011

‹ LEDs suspended from a tensile framework create intersecting volumes of light as they rotate.

⌐ The different configurations result in an assortment of illuminated conical and spherical shapes.

Eva Rucki, Conny Freyer and Sebastien Noel met
while studying at the Royal College of Art and founded
their multidisciplinary design practice, Troika, shortly
afterwards in 2003. Troika specialises in technology-
led installations and experiences that are often
influenced by established scientific principles relating
to light, sound, motion and natural phenomena, which
Troika reinterpret for the twenty-first century.

By transforming light into a seemingly tangible
entity, Thixotropes typifies Troika's ability to employ
cutting-edge technologies to create illusory effects.
The sculpture was originally commissioned by London
department store Selfridges to hang in its atrium over
the Christmas period and comprises eight mechanised
structures made from carbon rods that support angular
tensile arrangements of steel bands covered in a total
of 6,400 LEDs. The structures spin around their axes
at a speed of 360rpm, creating traces of light that
give the impression of intersecting geometric shapes.
Inspired by early motion capture experiments using
long-exposure photography, the installation translates
movement into an illusion of physicality that transcends
boundaries between art and science.

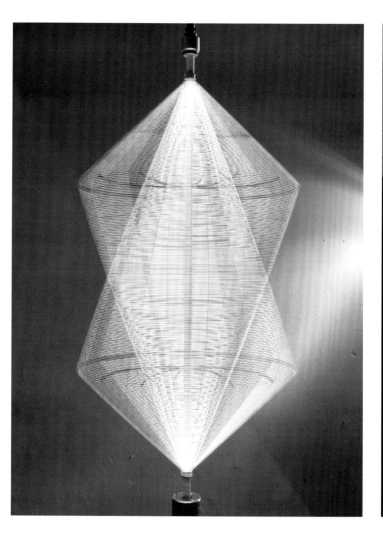

Product
Wallpiercing

Designer
Ron Gilad

Manufacturer
Flos

Date
2010

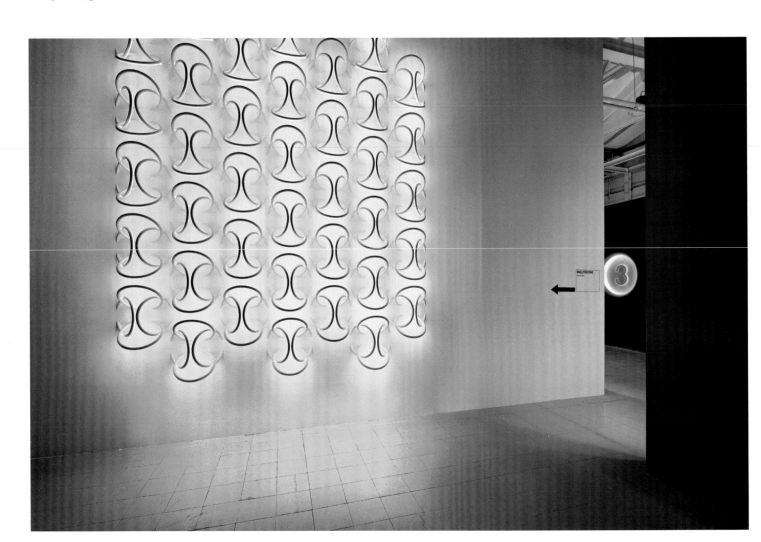

⌐ An aluminium hoop housing an array of LEDs can be arranged in interlocking patterns.

⌐ An RGB option enables coloured light across the full spectrum to be projected onto the wall.

At the 2010 Milan Furniture Fair, Italian brand Flos presented a radical collection of lighting fixtures that were seamlessly integrated into interior surfaces. Products from the Soft Architecture range can be embedded into walls and ceilings, recessed in smooth-edged sunken cavities or projecting outwards from the surface.

The standout product of the collection is Ron Gilad's futuristic Wallpiercing, which resembles an aluminium hoop lodged in the wall. An array of LEDs shielded by a polycarbonate diffuser on the inner surface projects light onto the wall, transforming the hooped form into a graphic silhouette. Individual units arranged in interlocking groups create a dramatic patchwork of light and shadow and can be programmed to display shifting patterns of colour.

Wallpiercing is designed to sit flush against the surface, with the electrical components housed within a shallow distribution box that can be built into the wall and plastered over. Soft Architecture illustrates how architecture and lighting are becoming increasingly connected, as innovative and efficient contemporary light sources merge with, or disappear into, the surrounding interior environment.

Product
SLAB

Designer
Johanna Grawunder

Manufacturer
**Carpenters
Workshop Gallery**

Date
2012

> SLAB transforms
from a mirrored surface
into a flat sheet of light.

∟ Grawunder's
installations explore how
light can merge with
interior architecture.

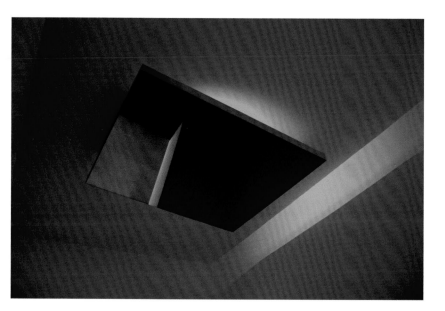

SLAB uses sophisticated LED technology to create a flat surface of light with a remarkably thin profile that can be integrated into existing interior architecture. During the day a mirrored plane reflects and augments the natural daylight in the space but when the light is turned on, the one-way mirror becomes a glowing surface. An array of high-powered LEDs combined with a system of filters and diffusers produces an even light across the entire surface. SLAB is suspended from the ceiling on a custom-designed cantilevered arm. Coloured light projects upwards, highlighting its ethereal presence.

Born in San Diego in 1961, Grawunder studied in California and Italy and spent several years working in the Milan studio of legendary Italian designer, Ettore Sottsass. She founded her own studio in 2001 and has completed several projects exploring how the physicality of light and colour can supplement the surroundings, including a series of 'light ceilings' that apply the same principles as SLAB to larger spaces within public or private institutions. SLAB is part of a limited edition collection designed for London–and Paris-based Carpenters Workshop Gallery.

Product
LED wallpaper

Designer
Ingo Maurer

Manufacturer
Architects Paper

Date
2007

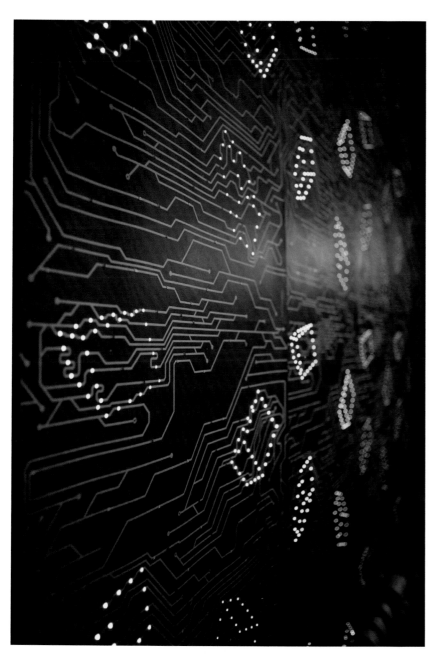

Ingo Maurer spent several years collaborating with a specialist wallpaper manufacturer to refine the technologies required to incorporate functioning LEDs into a flat surface. By combining a familiar product with a revolutionary manufacturing technique, the wallpaper epitomises Maurer's devotion to designing imaginative and technically challenging lighting products that give new technologies a poetic appeal.

The non-woven wallpaper is printed with a closed circuit of conductive paint before tiny LEDs are painstakingly fixed to the surface by hand using a specially developed conductive glue. Each 320cm x 60cm section is covered in a total of 840 light sources, arranged in five pattern repeats consisting of 48 white, 60 blue and 60 red LEDs. At the base of each length are a 12-volt ballast and a control unit that can be programmed to customise the patterns and adjust the brightness of the light. Conventional paste can be used to fix the paper to the wall and the electronics are hidden behind an aluminium skirting.

< Functioning LEDs attached to the surface of this wallpaper can be programmed to illuminate different patterns.

∧ It takes two days to glue the 840 LEDs to the printed circuit.

Product
**Circles and
Countercircles**

Designer
Troika

Date
2012

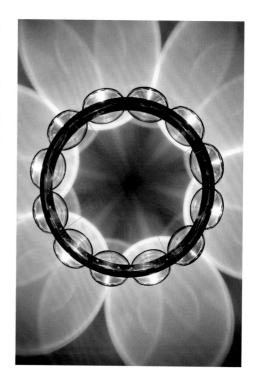

‹ Troika's chandeliers use centuries-old scientific principles to project diffused light onto the ceiling.

⌐ Small but powerful LED light sources are diffracted by a series of lenses.

Circles and Countercircles was the winning entry to a competition seeking lighting installations for the Royal Society of Arts headquarters in central London. Drawing on discoveries that took place during the Enlightenment period – particularly the works of Sir Isaac Newton and Augustin Fresnel – the chandelier mounted in the RSA's stairwell comprises a 1.2m diameter Fresnel lens that diffracts light directed at it from below by nine high-powered LEDs. The resulting pattern of overlapping spots resembles a traditional ceiling rose. In the Benjamin Franklin Room, an array of 12 Fresnel lenses encircles a polished aluminium ring that houses 12 high-powered LEDs and creates a dispersed geometric pattern.

These illusory interventions represent the evolution of the studio's ongoing exploration into the properties of light and optics. Troika has developed a series of evanescent artworks, including Lightrain (2010) and Falling Light (2011), which combine LEDs with lenses mounted on unidirectional mechanisms to project pools of light reminiscent of drops of water on the floor beneath them.

Product
Family of OLEDs

Designer
**Johanna
Schoemaker**

Date
2009

< The use of OLED panels
enables incredibly thin
surfaces to function as
light sources.

⌐ OLEDs are transparent
when turned off and can be
programmed to illuminate
sequentially to simulate
natural lighting conditions.

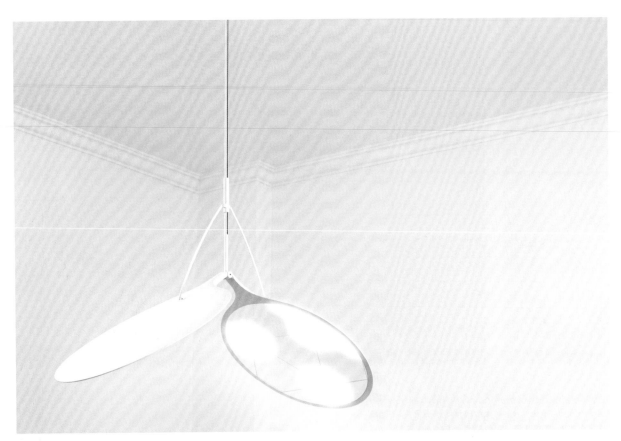

For her graduation project from the University of Wuppertal in Germany, Johanna Schoemaker developed a concept for a family of lamps that promote the inherent physical and practical advantages of OLED light sources. The slim forms occupy minimal visual and physical space, and accurate dimming options offer adaptable and dynamic lighting possibilities. The OLED panels covering the surfaces can be illuminated in a random sequence to simulate natural lighting effects, such as dappled sunlight shining through clouds, which Schoemaker's research suggests has psychological benefits.

The dispersion of light from the ceiling lamp can be adjusted by altering the opening angle using a touchscreen remote control, and the floor lamp is turned on using a sliding mechanism on the stand that opens it like an umbrella. The organic form and the opening action recall a flower unfurling its petals or an insect spreading its wings and offer a familiar point of reference that is often missing from products designed around new technologies.

Product	Designer	Manufacturer	Date
Flying Future	**Ingo Maurer**	**Ingo Maurer GmbH**	**2006**

L Flying Future is made from an undulating plastic surface covered in OLED panels.

The piece is designed to accentuate the lightness and transparency of OLEDs.

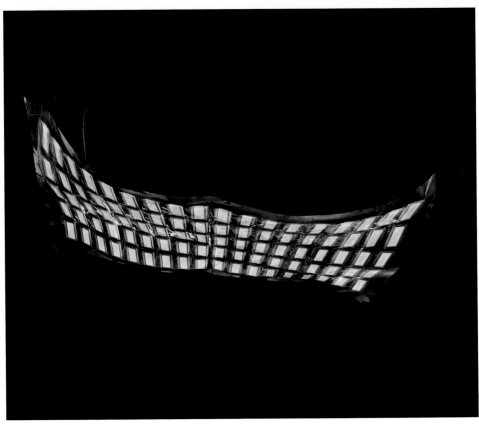

Ingo Maurer was one of the first designers to explore the formal and technical properties of OLED light sources and demonstrate potential applications for this emerging technology. As with his experimental LED products, Maurer's OLED designs do not attempt to hide the electronics and components that enable the product to function; instead these become part of the raw and futuristic aesthetic.

Maurer's first OLED projects were presented at the Milan Furniture Fair in 2006 and included a prototype of Flying Future. The luminaire is made from a rippling transparent surface suspended from sheer nylon threads and seems to float in the air. The OLED panels attached to the surface are transparent when unlit so the whole structure disappears against the background.

Impressed by the even quality of OLED light, which does not require a reflector to direct it or a separate diffuser, Maurer continues to collaborate with manufacturers on the development of ceiling and task lights that explore the suitability of these futuristic light sources in various scenarios.

Product	Designer	Manufacturer	Date
Edge	**Amanda Levete**	**Established & Sons**	**2010**

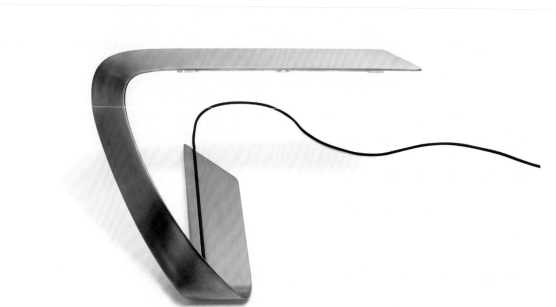

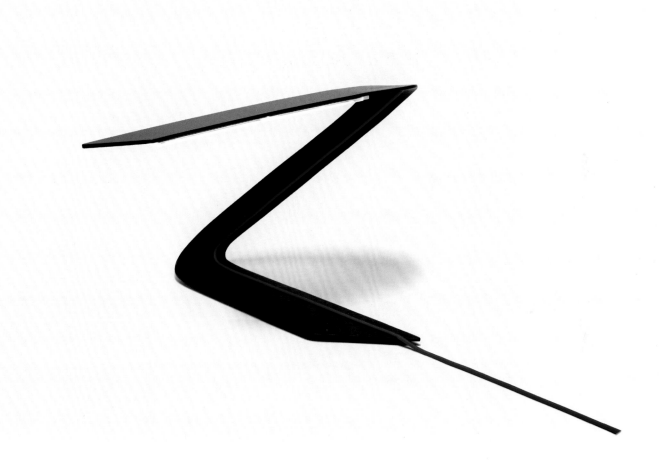

The futuristic form of this slender, sculptural object gives little indication of its function.

Downward facing OLED panels disperse a flat and even glow suitable for task lighting.

This task light by architect and designer Amanda Levete was developed in collaboration with Dutch electronics company Philips, which has encouraged several leading designers to demonstrate potential uses for its Lumiblade OLEDs. Levete is renowned for exploiting emerging technologies to facilitate radical spatial innovation, and the product's slimline and sinuous form emphasises the incredible thinness of the luminous panels. Two OLEDs – which have a mirror finish when turned off – are concealed on the underside of the uppermost section of a twisting ribbon of steel, giving the impression that light is emanating from the metal itself. The cantilevered form has a purity that is interrupted only by the addition of a coloured cable, which offers a clue as to the object's function.

The lamp demonstrates how the intelligent application of OLED technology will enable consumer lighting products to become smaller, slimmer and more refined, with fewer materials and components required to create attractive and effective solutions. The flat, even light that OLEDs produce means they are well suited to task lighting.

Product
Digital Dawn

Designer
Rachel Wingfield

Date
2000

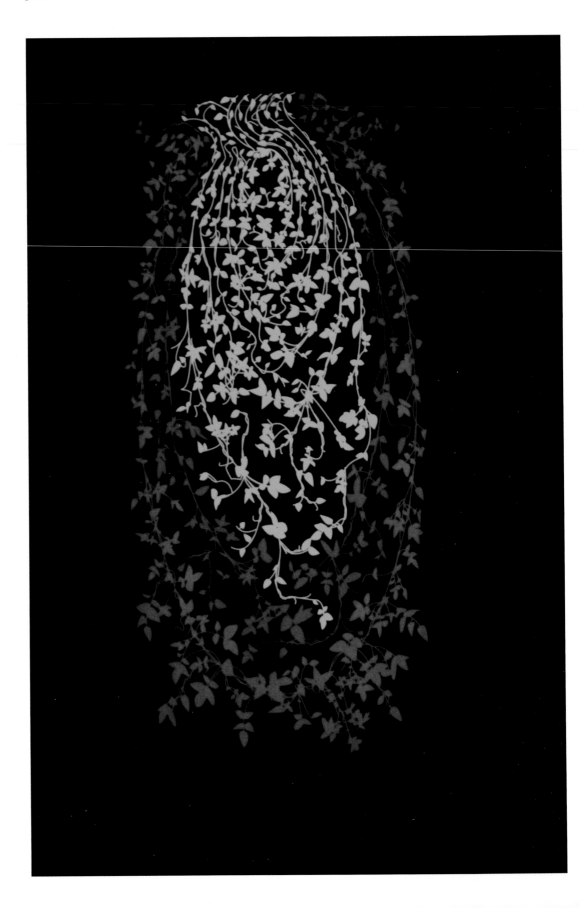

‹   Digital Dawn stores solar energy and emits a light that increases steadily as darkness falls.

›   A light sensor triggers a current that causes the printed electroluminescent surface of the blind to glow.

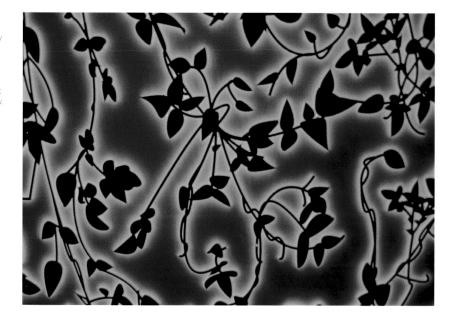

Digital Dawn is an intelligent window blind that responds to ambient light conditions by illuminating a foliage-inspired pattern as darkness falls. Designed by Rachel Wingfield during her studies at the Royal College of Art, the product mimics the natural process of photosynthesis, harvesting solar energy throughout the day and storing it, ready for the night. As the ambient light level drops, sensors built into the blind trigger a current that causes electrically conductive phosphorous inks to glow. The darker it becomes, the further the pattern spreads as the blind attempts to counteract the onset of darkness and maintain a balance in luminosity.

Wingfield's interest in the affect of light on our physiological condition led her to explore other applications for electroluminescent materials, including a pillow and duvet set with glowing fibres woven into the fabric that simulates a natural dawn and helps the user's body clock to recognise that it is time to wake up (Light Sleeper, 2001). Such applications for lighting technologies could help those who suffer from seasonal affective disorder and similar medical conditions.

Product
Daylight Entrance

Designer
Daniel Rybakken

Date
2008-10

⌐ Daylight Entrance gives the impression of daylight streaming through a window onto the wall.

L Light is projected onto the inside of the surface by a panel of recessed LEDs.

This installation, in the entrance hallway of a property company in Stockholm, Sweden, gives the impression that daylight is falling onto the wall, despite the fact that there is no source of natural light in the space. To create the illusion, a trapezoidal section is accurately milled out of a solid Corian® panel, and a metal sheet covered in LEDs is placed in the cavity so light penetrates the remaining surface. Several panels containing more than 6,000 LEDs are incorporated into walls throughout the building's circulation areas, bringing the sensation of daylight into these otherwise gloomy spaces.

Norwegian designer Daniel Rybakken is interested in the psychological benefits of sunlight and in ways of artificially replicating the sensation of daylight indoors. Daylight Entrance is the result of Rybakken's iterative exploration of this principle, which began with a project called Daylight Comes Sideways (2007) that used LEDs to project a blurry image of trees moving in the wind onto a semi-transparent surface.

Product
Airborne Collection

Designer
Hussein Chalayan

Date
2007

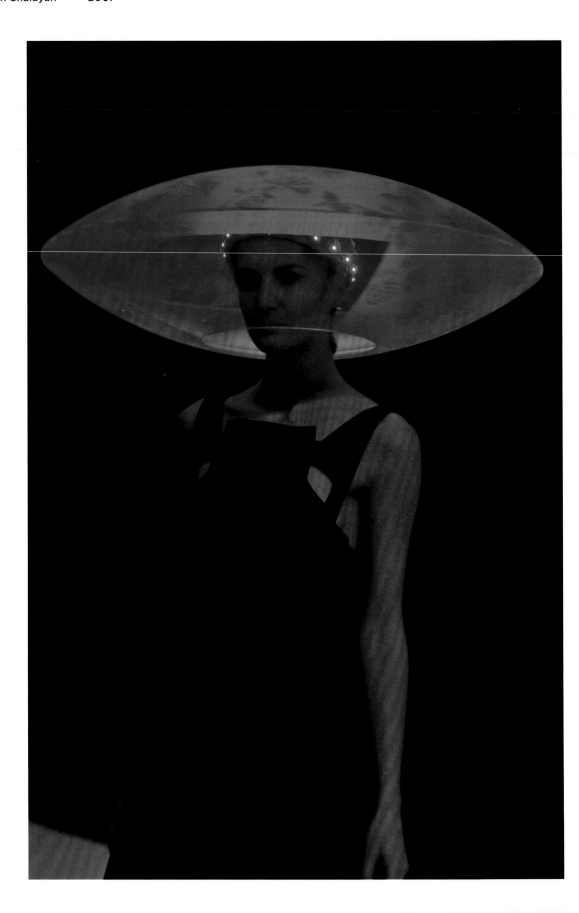

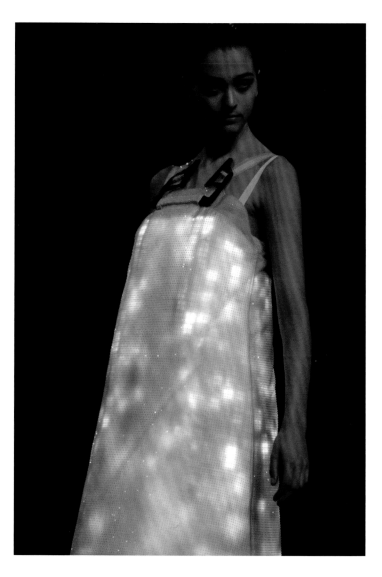

Taking advantage of the lightweight properties of LEDs and their ability to be charged using portable power sources, Cypriot fashion designer Hussein Chalayan embedded light sources into several high-tech garments that dazzled audiences at his 2007 Autumn/Winter catwalk show. The Airborne collection is themed around the changing seasons and the distinctive properties of light and weather at different times of the year. To combat the darkness of winter, domed headpieces fitted with red LEDs illuminate a floral pattern on the transparent surface. In contrast, a dress designed to evoke the brightness and optimism of spring combines Swarovski crystals with 15,600 LEDs that display fluctuating patterns of coloured light across its surface.

Taking inspiration from architecture and science, Chalayan's collections use technology to produce show-stopping effects involving light and movement, while achieving an essential formal elegance through their refined tailoring. Electronics specialist Moritz Waldemeyer helped to engineer and programme the integrated lighting systems.

‹ A row of red LEDs produces a warm glow on the surface of a futuristic headdress.

ʌ Thousands of LEDs combine with Swarovski crystal displays to illuminate the surface of this dress with a shimmering abstract pattern.

Product
Pixel Cloud

Designer
**Jason Bruges
Studio**

Date
2007

‹   Pixel Cloud consists
of 624 spheres that each
act as individual pixels in a
three-dimensional matrix.

›   Shifting patterns
of colour represent the
changing weather outside.

Jason Bruges Studio works across art, architecture
and branding to produce engaging, interactive
installations that often use light to communicate
information. Extending over eight storeys in the
atrium of an international law firm in London, Pixel
Cloud acts as a real-time simulation of the position
of the sun and clouds passing above the building that
plays out on a three-dimensional matrix consisting
of 624 translucent polycarbonate globes – or pixels.

A camera on the building's roof takes pictures
of the sky and sends these to a central server that
translates the images into a special code. This code
controls the light output from 24 LEDs inside each
of the translucent spheres. A custom-made
dodecahedron-shaped circuit board powers the
LEDs, creating a smooth transition between different
colours and an even light across the globe's surface.

The responsive sculpture is arranged in a grid
that mirrors the composition of the building's façade.
Information about the weather at the company's offices
around the world can also be received by RSS feed
and displayed by Pixel Cloud, creating a sense of
interaction on a global scale.

Product
SNOG Chelsea

Designer
Cinimod Studio

Date
2010

∧ A ceiling of rippling
panels developed using
parametric software
displays a shifting pattern
of coloured light.

> A soft pastel palette is
achieved by using RGBW
light sources.

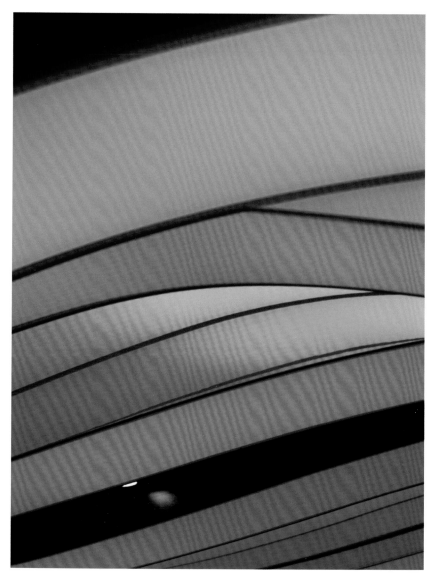

When frozen yoghurt retailer SNOG invited regular collaborator Cinimod Studio to develop an interior scheme for its store in Chelsea, London, the designers turned to LED lighting to create a scheme that augments the brand's playful identity and delivers an eye-catching street presence. To ensure a good level of light throughout the narrow interior, Cinimod Studio concealed more than 400 strips of LED lights behind undulating panels that stretch the entire length of the store. The LED strips house RGBW light sources, which include white lights as well as the typical red, green and blue palette to enable less intense shades to be produced. The continuously shifting pattern of pastel-coloured light displayed on the ceiling is linked to the store's sound system and responds to the tempo and vibrancy of the music.

LED products have been used across the store's lighting, from the coloured ceiling to white task lights and the fascia lighting. The result is an energy-efficient and fully controllable lighting setup that can be dimmed or brightened as required throughout the day.

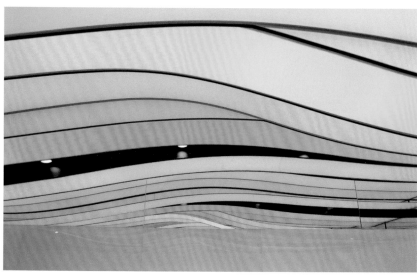

Product
Awakening Lamp

Designer
Front

Date
2003

⌄ The lamp slumps on
the floor when no one
is around.

⌐ Motion sensors prompt
the lamp to spring up when
someone comes near.

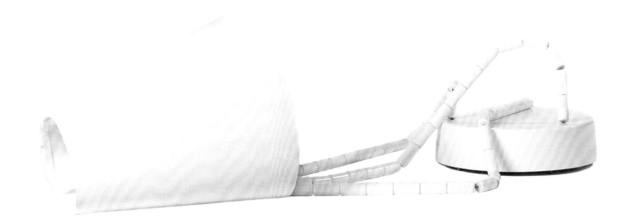

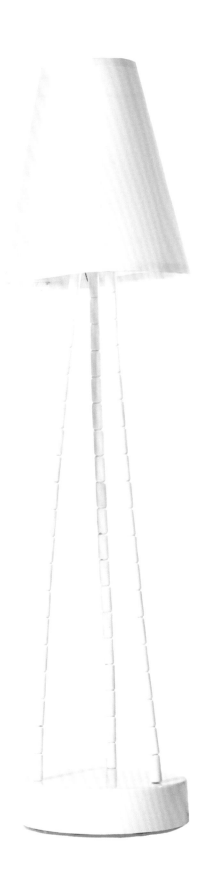

Front was founded in 2003 by four graduates from the University College of Arts, Crafts and Design (Konstfack) in Stockholm, Sweden. Sofia Lagerkvist, Charlotte von der Lancken, Anna Lindgren and Katja Sävström (who has since left the group) studied together in the university's industrial design programme where they set about developing their own brand of experimental design, becoming renowned for allowing random factors such as the behaviour of animals or the forces generated by an explosion to influence the outcome of their projects.

Awakening Lamp is part of an early collection called Design by that includes objects with built-in behaviours that respond to their environment. The lamp uses a motion sensor to detect the presence of someone entering the room, which causes it to spring to attention and switch on automatically. When no one is around the light turns off and slumps to the floor. The Design by series helped establish Front at the vanguard of concept-led design, which they have continued to explore through commercial projects for companies including Kartell, IKEA and Moooi.

Product	Designer	Manufacturer	Date
Self Portrait	**rAndom International**	**Carpenters Workshop Gallery**	**2010**

L Self Portrait senses when someone is standing in front of it and reproduces their image on a light reactive ultraviolet surface.

> The portrait fades away in a few minutes so there is no lasting record of the encounter.

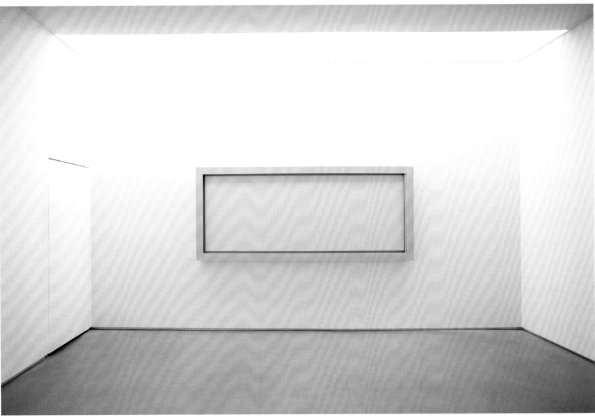

Using a small camera hidden in the frame, Self Portrait captures an image of whoever is in front of it and 'prints' his or her portrait onto a light-reactive canvas. The camera is triggered by movement, and Self Portrait transfers the picture onto its surface using a large LED print head that scans along the length of the frame. The image left behind gradually fades away, leaving the frame empty and ready to create its next portrait.

rAndom International was founded by Stuart Wood, Florian Ortkrass and Hannes Koch, who met at Brunel University and went on to complete postgraduate studies at the Royal College of Art. Among their earliest projects were Temporary Graffiti and Lightroller (both 2005), which feature surfaces made from a photochromic material that reacts to the presence of light, creating a visual trace that lasts for just a few minutes. These principles developed into a series of Temporary Printing Machines produced as limited edition artworks. Self Portrait defies the notion of the portrait as a permanent record and instead produces an ephemeral representation of a moment that is soon lost forever.

Product	Designer	Manufacturer	Date
Lolita	**Ron Arad**	**Swarovski**	**2004**

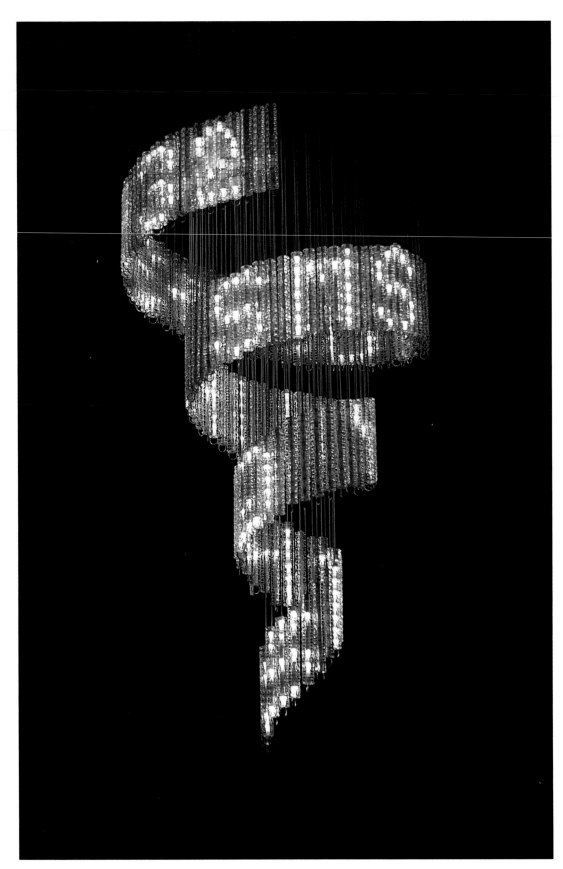

L Text messages sent to a special number scroll across the glittering surface of the chandelier.

〉 The components are suspended from 1,000 metres of cabling.

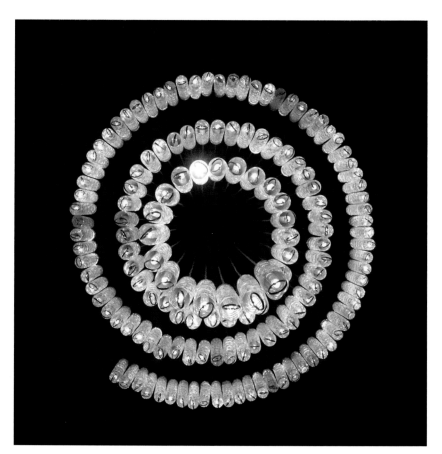

Each year since 2002, crystal manufacturer Swarovski has invited some of the world's leading designers to create innovative chandeliers using cut crystal in its myriad forms. The annual Swarovski Crystal Palace presentation is a landmark event on the design calendar and has established the brand – which makes most of its money from crystal giftware, jewellery and industrial optical equipment – as a powerful player on the art and design scene.

Ron Arad's dramatic interactive chandelier was presented at the Milan Furniture Fair in 2004 and consists of 2,100 Swarovski crystals separated by white LEDs that are programmed to display scrolling text messages sent to a dedicated phone number. Anyone who has the number can send an SMS that is relayed to a series of processors, which then translate the text into pixel data used to illuminate the LEDs. The descending spiral of crystal references the form of traditional chandeliers that might be found in the centre of a grand staircase, but the technology required to design and manufacture this sophisticated and interactive sculpture belongs firmly in the twenty-first century.

Product	Designer	Manufacturer	Date
You Fade to Light	**rAndom International**	**Carpenters Workshop Gallery**	**2009**

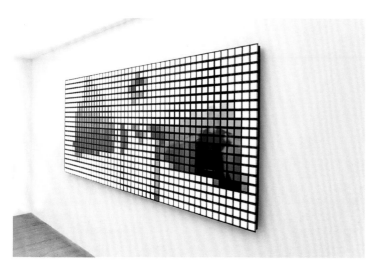

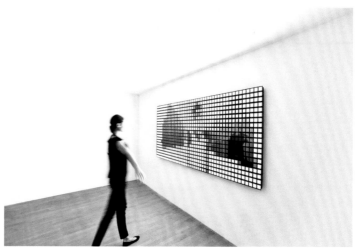

‹ The surface of OLED panels mirrors movement occurring in front of it.

⌐ Motion-tracking software switches the panels on and off to create a responsive image.

You Fade to Light was originally commissioned by Dutch electronics brand Philips, which invited rAndom International to experiment with its Lumiblade OLED technology in an artistic context. It comprises several hundred OLED panels arranged as a thin floating screen that resembles a mosaic of mirrored tiles when unlit. The piece comes to life when somebody steps in front of it, and his or her movements are recorded by a tracking camera hidden in the centre of the surface. Custom-designed software instantaneously translates this information into a dynamic pixellated image. The viewer's actions are mirrored by the illuminated panels, which turn on and off accordingly.

The reactive nature of You Fade to Light is typical of rAndom International's work, which endeavours to identify new forms of interaction between people and objects, using technology. Similar processes informed the development of Swarm Light (2010), a suspended matrix of LEDs that responds to nearby noises by sending a flickering pattern of light resembling the flocking behaviour of birds or insects across its surface, and Future Self (2012), which projects a three-dimensional image of the viewers onto a column of LED-covered poles.

Product
Bourrasque

Designer
Paul Cocksedge

Date
2011

∧   This temporary
installation resembles a
stack of paper that seems
to have exploded from the
municipal offices of Lyon's
City Hall into the seventeenth
century courtyard.

The double-sided
electroluminescent sheets
are suspended from a
delicate and almost
invisible structure.

For the 2011 edition of the annual Festival of Light in Lyon, France, Paul Cocksedge designed this poetic installation consisting of 200 glowing sheets that appear to have been launched into the sky by a huge gust of wind. The A3-sized sheets are made from a thin, double-sided electroluminescent material that glows when a current passes through it. Each piece is moulded by hand into a curved form and then suspended in a stream that reaches a height of over 15 metres.

Bourrasque represents an exploration of a material that combines the properties of paper and light; raising questions about the future of written media in the face of digital devices, such as tablets and electronic paper. The previous year, Cocksedge installed a similar paper-inspired artwork in a hallway of London's Victoria and Albert Museum. Comprised of numbered sheets of curled Corian®, this piece was in place for just one day before the sheets were given away to be used as individual paper trays.

Product
Tree

Designer
Simon Heijdens

Date
2004

Motion sensors provoke the projection of a tree to shed its leaves when people pass by.

The leaves on the ground stir when they are disturbed by movement.

Tree is a responsive installation that changes throughout the day and symbolises the decline of nature in the urban environment. A large tree is projected in white light onto the façade of a building, its branches and leaves moving in response to live measurements of the surrounding wind conditions. When someone passes the tree, a leaf falls to the ground nearby, and the leaves that have been shed gradually accumulate and illuminate a section of the street. The shapes projected onto the ground stir and swirl when people walk through them, and the next day the tree regenerates and the process begins again.

Dutch designer Simon Heijdens studied filmmaking in Berlin before enrolling in the product design course at Design Academy Eindhoven, and his background in film clearly influences the narrative quality and transient nature of his design projects. By combining cutting-edge digital technology with natural iconography, Heijdens creates organically evolving experiences that manage to be simultaneously novel, intuitive and poetic.

Product
Sonumbra

Designer
**Rachel Wingfield
and Mathias
Gmachl/Loop.pH**

Date
2006

< The lacework canopy of Sonumbra is made from electroluminescent fibres that light up when people approach.

⌐ Movement around the installation produces a dynamic response of light and sound.

Sonumbra is a large parasol woven from a tensile lacework of electroluminescent fibres that responds to the movement of people in its vicinity by sending a pattern of light flowing in their direction across its delicate surface. Rachel Wingfield and Mathias Gmachl, who founded design studio Loop.pH in 2003, initially developed the project in response to a commission for a site-specific light installation at an arts festival in Sunderland, England. Bespoke versions were subsequently produced for specific exhibitions, and an aural dimension was added so the visitor's presence provokes a reaction of rhythms, harmonies and light.

An omnidirectional camera housed in the supportive mast captures the activity of people near the parasol, and specially developed software translates this into a pulsing pattern that emanates from the base and spreads across the lace-like canopy, which is virtually invisible when unlit. The designers believe Sonumbra has the potential to be used in developing countries to provide shelter from the sun during the day, while harvesting the energy required to supply illumination in areas without electricity when darkness falls.

Product
Volume

Designer
UnitedVisualArtists

Date
2006

⌃ Volume consists of
48 LED-covered columns
fitted with speakers.

⌐ The movement of
visitors around the columns
triggers patterns of noise
and light.

UnitedVisualArtists (UVA) is a multidisciplinary practice whose work exists in the space between sculpture, architecture, live performance and digital installation. Their initial experiences creating groundbreaking performance visuals for live events informed their expansion into the fields of digital sculpture and temporary and permanent installations. These projects engage users by reacting to their presence and creating a sense of shared experience. UVA is one of several digital design practices exploiting the interactive potential of sensor-based systems to control the behaviour of lighting and sound.

Volume is an installation comprising 48 luminous and sound-emitting columns that respond to movement by creating an immersive visual and aural environment. LEDs covering the front and back of the columns produce shifting and pulsing patterns of light, and a speaker fitted to each column emits a sound when movement is detected nearby. These notes contribute to a mesmeric layered soundscape composed by experimental electronic musicians Massive Attack. First presented in the garden of London's Victoria and Albert Museum in 2006, Volume subsequently travelled to Hong Kong, Taiwan, Melbourne and St Petersburg.

Product
OUTRACE

Designer
**KRAM/
WEISSHAAR**

Date
2010

‹ Eight industrial robots were adapted to write messages in the air with light.

› LEDs fitted to the arms left traces that were recorded by long exposure cameras.

Throughout the duration of the 2010 London Design Festival, visitors to Trafalgar Square were confronted with the spectacle of eight industrial robots, borrowed from car manufacturer Audi's production line, writing messages with light in the night air. German design studio KRAM/WEISSHAAR invited the public to upload messages onto the project's website, which were then translated into data that directed the robots' movement. A powerful LED light source on the end of each robot's tool head produced traces that were recorded by a series of long exposure cameras and collated into a video displaying the entire message.

A 1KW server capable of handling over 10,000 messages in a week processed a film every 60 seconds and disseminated them through the project's website and directly on YouTube.

Clemens Weisshaar and Reed Kram's work predominantly focuses on finding new ways to harness advanced software systems to create engaging forms of interaction between people and products. OUTRACE presents technology in a dramatic and participatory format, based around two universally recognisable entities: language and light.

Product
Solar Tree

Designer
Ross Lovegrove

Manufacturer
Artemide

Date
2006–2010

‹ Solar Tree combines
self-sustaining street
lighting with a circular
concrete bench, creating
a focal point in the urban
environment.

› The slender steel
stalks reach a height of
5.5 metres and are capped
with LED lights.

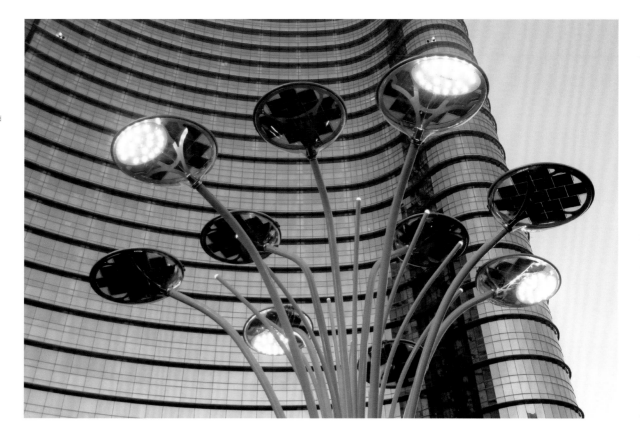

Solar Tree was developed by British designer Ross
Lovegrove and Italian lighting brand Artemide to prove
that attractive, self-sustaining street lighting could
be manufactured and installed in the public domain.
Inspired by the process of photosynthesis and the
beauty of natural forms, Solar Tree is intended to
act as a beacon in the urban landscape.

Lovegrove's trademark organic aesthetic lends
Solar Tree a sculptural presence, with some of the
grass-like stems ending in a 1W LED and others capped
with petal-like heads. Solar panels on the top surface
of these heads translate the sun's energy into voltage
to power the array of downward facing LEDs that
deliver a light output of 1250 lumen. Solar Tree can
function autonomously – with the solar panels charging
batteries in the base to power the lights when dusk
arrives – or can be plugged into the public electricity
grid, feeding surplus energy back into the mainframe.

Product
Speed of Light

Designer
NVA

Date
2012

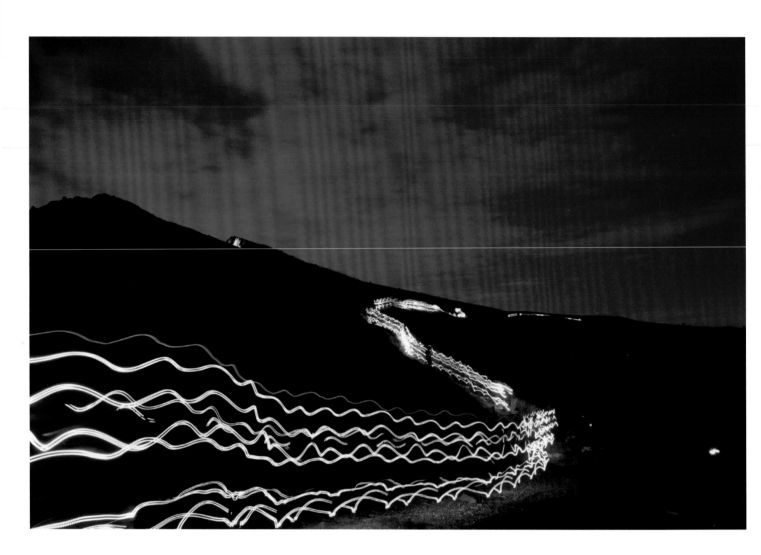

∧ Speed of Light was a
mass participatory artwork
involving runners wearing
LED-covered light suits.

‹ The pulsing lights
created rhythmic patterns
on the hillside as the runners
moved in choreographed
sequence.

The interactive and performative possibilities enabled
by new lighting technologies have stimulated an increase
in the number of site-specific lighting installations and
citywide lighting festivals, such as Lyon's Festival of
Light and the Lumiere festival in Durham, England.
During the 2012 Edinburgh International Festival,
Scottish arts charity NVA (which is an acronym for
nacionale vitae activa, a Latin phrase meaning 'the
right to influence public affairs') instigated a participatory
lighting installation by dressing hundreds of runners in
LED-covered suits and coordinating a choreographed
performance on the side of the mountain that
overlooks the city.

Each night during the festival, an audience carrying
their own portable light sources was guided to a vantage
point on top of Arthur's Seat, from which they could
observe the performers running and moving in
sequence along the paths that criss-cross the dark
landscape. The light suits pulsed and flickered with
programmed patterns of coloured light, uniting the
performers and evoking the shimmering lights of the
city in the background. Speed of Light fulfilled NVA's
remit to promote collaborative art that engages its
audience by using light and human motion as the basis
for a unique and memorable participatory event.

Product
BIX

Designer
realities:united

Date
2003

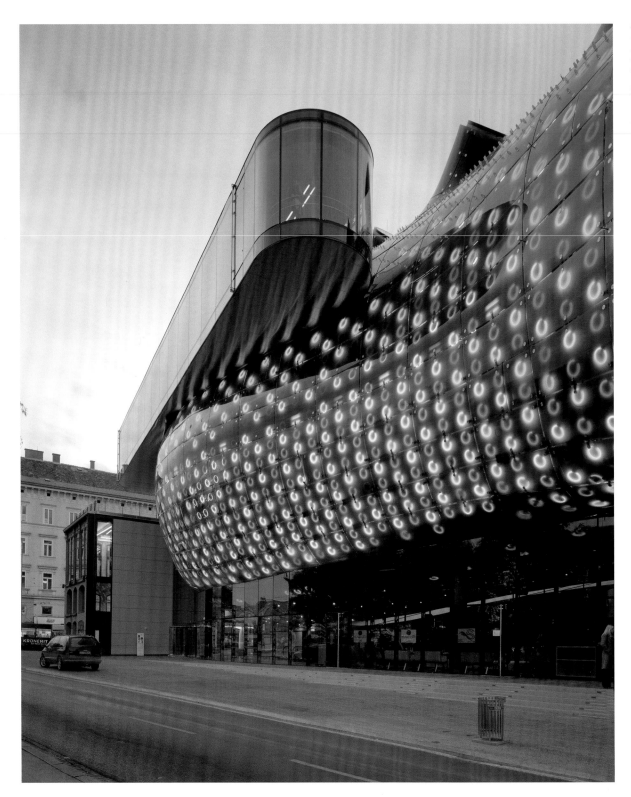

‹ A matrix of
fluorescent tubes acts
as a three-dimensional
display for specially
commissioned artworks.

› The resolution of the
images is restricted by the
number of lamps that could
fit on the building's façade.

At night the undulating façade of the Kunsthaus Graz art gallery in Switzerland becomes a three-dimensional display illuminated by 930 circular fluorescent tubes built into the space behind the building's glossy Plexiglass skin. The biomorphic building was designed by architects Peter Cook and Colin Fournier, but the lighting installation was added only when technical and financial constraints forced changes to be made to the river-facing façade, which was originally planned to offer limited views of the interior.

Tasked with resurrecting the functional potential of the transparent cladding, Berlin-based art and architecture studio realities:united decided to develop a permanent lighting installation. They chose an established light source rather than an untested new technology that might not be as dependable. Special software was developed that enables the brightness of the fluorescent lamps to be adjusted at a rate of 18 frames per second, making them suitable for displaying video and animations. The artworks shown on the façade are restricted to monochrome images with a low resolution; however, BIX has succeeded as a platform for expanding the gallery's programme into the realm of digital media and has established a dialogue between the building and the surrounding urban environment.

Product
**Dream Cube
Shanghai Corporate
Pavilion**

Designer
ESI Design

Date
2010

< Pulsing LEDs
illuminated the façade of
the Dream Cube at the
Shanghai World Expo.

⌐ The movement of
visitors inside a circular
theatre stimulated shifting
patterns of light on the
building's exterior.

As visitors approached the Shanghai Corporate
Pavilion at the 2010 World Expo hosted by the Chinese
city, they encountered a 40,000-square-foot structure
pulsing with coloured light. Known as the Dream Cube,
the project was the result of a collaboration between
US experience design firm ESI Design and Chinese
architecture practice Atelier FCJZ. They produced
a seamless experience where the building's LED
exterior – comprising of millions of recycled
transparent polycarbonate rods – glimmered and
changed in response to interactive activities within
the building.

Visitors were led through a series of multimedia
experiences telling the story of Shanghai's past,
present and future, towards a circular theatre where
a 360-degree projection celebrated the city's sights
and sounds and encouraged the visitors to clap and
wave their hands in unison. These actions were
captured by motion sensors connected to a control
system that translated the movement into patterns
of light on the pavilion's surface. The Dream Cube's
reactive light façade acted as a metaphor for the
collaborative action required to generate positive
change within the urban environment.

Product
Showtime

Designer
**Jason Bruges
Studio**

Date
2010

⌐ A panoramic
representation of the
London skyline is played
out in lights on the façade
of the W Hotel.

❯ The changing colours
reflect the time of year
and activity in the
surrounding area.

The façade of the W Hotel in London's Leicester Square is wrapped in a veil of fritted glass, behind which 600 lights recreate the shifting colours of the surrounding skyline. Eight cameras on the roof of the hotel take a picture every minute throughout the day, and these images are then stitched together to create a panoramic film. The film is translated into a dynamic pattern using specially designed software and condensed into a two-minute performance to be displayed continuously across the surface of the 10-storey building when darkness falls. Visitors never experience the same presentation twice, as the installation constantly changes in response to the seasons and events taking place in its vicinity.

The designers used LED tube lights to achieve smooth transitions between different colours of light. These products are able to produce subtle pastel shades that distinguish the performative façade from the bright neon surrounding the building, which is situated in the heart of London's premiere filmic location. The lights are also weatherproof and four times more efficient than their neon counterparts.

Directory of Designers and Manufacturers

Designers	Website	Designers	Website
Omer Arbel	www.omerarbel.com	Alexander Taylor	www.alexandertaylor.com
Hussein Chalayan	www.husseinchalayan.com	Lonneke Gordijn and Ralph Nauta	www.studiodrift.com
Ross Lovegrove	www.rosslovegrove.com	Johanna Schoemaker	www.johannaschoemaker.com
Front	www.designfront.org	Ron Arad	www.ronarad.co.uk
Geoffrey Mann	www.mrmann.co.uk	Zaha Hadid	www.zaha-hadid.com
Marcel Wanders	www.marcelwanders.com	Jasper Morrison	www.jaspermorrison.com
Tom Dixon	www.tomdixon.net	Philippe Starck	www.starck.com
realities:united	www.realities-united.de	Nendo	www.nendo.jp
Tord Boontje	www.tordboontje.com	Benjamin Hubert	www.benjaminhubert.co.uk
Autoban	www.autoban212.com	Marcus Tremonto	www.treluce.com
Ferruccio Laviani	www.laviani.com	Francisco Gomez Paz	www.gomezpaz.com
Paul Cocksedge	www.paulcocksedgestudio.com	Paolo Rizzatto	www.paolorizzatto.it
Freshwest	www.freshwest.co.uk	Antonio Citterio	www.antoniocitterioandpartners.it
Patricia Urquiola	www.patriciaurquiola.com	Toan Nguyen	www.toannguyenstudio.com
Eliana Gerotto	www.elianagerotto.com	Yves Béhar	www.fuseproject.com
Troika	www.troika.uk.com	Pieke Bergmans	www.piekebergmans.com
Matali Crasset	www.matalicrasset.com	Jurgen Bey	www.studiomakkinkbey.nl
Jake Dyson	www.jakedyson.com	Andreas Engesvik	www.andreasengesvik.no
Ron Gilad	www.rongilad.com	Ronan and Erwan Bouroullec	www.bouroullec.com
Daniel Rybakken	www.danielrybakken.com	Janne Kyttanen	www.jannekyttanen.com
Lee Broom	www.leebroom.com	Olafur Eliasson	www.olafureliasson.net
Rachel Wingfield /Loop.pH	www.loop.ph	VW+BS	www.vwbs.co.uk
ESI Design	www.esidesign.com	Mortiz Waldemeyer	www.waldemeyer.com
Mattias Ståhlbom /TAF	www.tafarkitektkontor.se	Luca Nichetto	www.lucanichetto.com
Amanda Levete	www.ala.uk.com	Gianpietro Gai	www.genikdisegno.it
Ingo Maurer	www.ingo-maurer.com	KRAM/WEISSHAAR	www.kramweisshaar.com
Luc Merx	www.gagat.com	Ed Carpenter	www.edcarpenter.co.uk
Atelier Van Lieshout	www.ateliervanlieshout.com	Herzog & de Meuron	www.herzogdemeuron.com
Industrial Facility	www.industrialfacility.co.uk	Jason Bruges Studio	www. jasonbruges.com

Designers	Website	Manufacturers	Website
Inga Sempé	www.ingasempe.fr	Bocci	www.bocci.ca
Samuel Wilkinson	www.samuelwilkinson.com	Yamagiwa	www.yamagiwa-lighting.com
Hulger	www.hulger.com	Moooi	www.moooi.com
Raimond Puts	www.moooi.com	Flos	www.flos.com
Bertjan Pot	www.bertjanpot.nl	Swarovski Crystal Palace	www.swarovskicrystalpalace.com
Julia Lohmann	www.julialohmann.co.uk	De La Espada	www.delaespada.com
rAndom International	www.random-international.com	Kartell	www.kartell.it
Johanna Grawunder	www.grawunder.com	Foscarini	www.foscarini.com
Cinimod Studio	www.cinimodstudio.com	Artemide	www.artemide.com
NVA	www.nva.org.uk	Danese	www.danesemilano.com
Sebastian Wrong	www.thewrongshop.co.uk	Meta	www.madebymeta.com
Chris Kabel	www.chriskabel.com	Muuto	www.muuto.com
Barber Osgerby	www.barberosgerby.com	Established & Sons	www.establishedandsons.com
Stuart Haygarth	www.stuarthaygarth.com	Materialise.MGX	www.mgxbymaterialise.com
Charles Trevelyan	www.charlestrevelyan.com	Droog	www.droog.com
Marc Sadler	www.marcsadler.it	Luceplan	www.luceplan.com
Sylvain Willenz	www.sylvainwillenz.com	Herman Miller	www.hermanmiller.com
Victor Vetterlein	www.victorvetterlein.com	Asplund	www.asplund.org
Simon Heijdens	www.simonheijdens.com	Fontana Arte	www.fontanaarte.com
Ilse Crawford	www.studioilse.com	Thorsten van Elten	www.thorstenvanelten.com
Claesson Koivisto Rune	www.ckr.se	iGuzzini	www.iguzzini.com
UVA	www.uva.co.uk/	Cappellini	www.cappellini.it
		Hulger	www.hulger.com
		&tradition	www.andtradition.com
		Wästberg	www.wastberg.com

Image credits

Form

Genesy
Photograph by Ingmar Kurth. Courtesy of Artemide GmbH. Genesy, Zaha Hadid © Artemide GmbH.

Genesy
Photograph by Ingmar Kurth. Courtesy of Artemide GmbH. Genesy, Zaha Hadid © Artemide GmbH.

Mercury
Photograph by Fabian Auyrel Hild. Courtesy of Artemide GmbH. Mercury, Ross Lovegrove © Artemide GmbH.

Pipe
Photograph © Miro Zagnoli. Courtesy of Artemide Gmbh. Pipe, Herzog and de Meuron © Artemide GmbH.

Pipe
Photograph by Linus Lintner. Courtesy of Artemide Gmbh. Pipe, Herzog and de Meuron © Artemide GmbH.

Spun Light
Courtesy of Flos SpA. Spun Light, Sebastian Wrong © Flos.

Spun Light
Photograph by Santi Caleca. Courtesy of Flos. Spun Light, Sebastian Wrong © Flos.

Loop
Courtesy of Fontana Arte SpA. Loop, Voon Wong and Benson Saw © Fontana Arte SpA.

O-Space
Courtesy of Foscarini SRL. O Space, Giampietro Gai and Luca Nichetto © Foscarini SRL.

Andromeda
Courtesy of Yamagiwa Corporation. Andromeda, Ross Lovegrove © Yamagiwa Corporation.

PizzaKobra
Photograph by Amendolaggine e Barracchia. Courtesy of iGuzzini illuminazione SpA. PizzaKobra, Ron Arad © iGuzzini illuminazione SpA.

Leaf
Courtesy of Herman Miller. Leaf lamp, Yves Behar © Herman Miller.

FL/Y
Courtesy of Kartell SpA. FL/Y, Ferruccio Laviani, Kartell © Kartell SpA.

Blossom
Design by Studio Tord Boontje for Swarovski. Blossom, Tord Boontje © Studio Tord Boontje.

Family Lamp
Courtesy of Carpenters Workshop Gallery. Family Lamp, Atelier van Lieshout © Carpenters Workshop Gallery/ Mondrian Ltd.

Light Blubs
Photograph by Mirjam Bleeker. Courtesy of Pieke Bergmans, www.piekebergmans. com/info@piekebergmans.com. Light Blubs, Pieke Bergmans © Pieke Bergmans

Titanic Lamp
Photograph by George Ong. Courtesy of Charles Trevelyan. Titanic Lamp, Charles Trevelyan © Charles Trevelyan.

Titanic Lamp
Courtesy of Charles Trevelyan. Titanic Lamp, Charles Trevelyan © Charles Trevelyan

Bourgie
Courtesy of Kartell SpA. Bourgie, Ferruccio Laviani, Kartell © Kartell SpA

Skygarden
Courtesy of Flos SpA. Skygarden, Marcel Wanders, Flos © Flos SpA.

Gun Lamp
Courtesy of Flos SpA. Gun Lamp, Philippe Starck, Flos © Flos SpA.

Pigeon Light
Courtesy of Thorsten Van Elten. Pigeon Light, Ed Carpenter © Thorsten Van Elten.

Animal Lamps
Courtesy of Moooi. Animal lamps, Front © Moooi.

Dear Ingo
Courtesy of Moooi. Dear Ingo, Ron Gilad © Moooi.

Garland
Courtesy of Artecnica. Garland, Tord Boontje © Artecnica.

Caboche
Courtesy of Foscarini SRL. Caboche lamp, Patricia Urquiola and Eliana Gerotto © Foscarini SRL.

Booklamp
Courtesy of De La Espada. Booklamp, Autoban © Autoban.

Tab
Courtesy of Barber Osgerby Studio. Tab Light, Barber Osgerby. Flos © Barber Osgerby Studio.

Piani
Courtesy of Studio Bouroullec. Piani, Ronan and Erwan Bouroullec, Flos © Studio Bouroullec.

E27
Courtesy of Muuto. E27, Mattias Ståhlbom, Muuto © Muuto.

Maki
Courtesy of Foscarini SRL. Maki, Nendo © Foscarini SRL.

Ge-Off Sphere
Courtesy of Ron Arad Associates. Ge Off Sphere, Ron Arad © Ron Arad Associates.

LILY.MGX
Lily.MGX designed by Janne Kyttanen for .MGX by Materialise. Lily.MGX, Janne Kyttanen © Materialise.

Attracted to Light
Photograph by Sylvain Deleu. Courtesy of Geoffrey Mann. Attracted to Light, Geoffrey Mann © Geoffrey Mann.

Fall of the Damned
Courtesy of Luc Merx. Fall of the Damned, Luc Merx © Luc Merx.

Materials

Tide
Courtesy of Stuart Haygarth. Tide, Stuart Haygarth © Stuart Haygarth.

Ruminant Bloom
Courtesy of Julia Lohmann Studio. Ruminant Bloom, Julia Lohmann © Julia Lohmann

Rough Diamond collection
Courtesy of Lee Broom. Rough Diamond, Lee Broom © Lee Broom.

Light Shade Shade
Photograph by Peer Lindgreen. Courtesy of Moooi. Light Shade Shade, Jurgen Bey © Moooi.

Light Shade Shade
Photograph by Nicole Marnati. Courtesy of Moooi. Light Shade Shade, Jurgen Bey © Moooi.

Decanterlight
Courtesy of Lee Broom. Decanterlight, Lee Broom © Lee Broom.

Trash Me VV1
Courtesy of &tradition. Trash Me VV1, Victor Vetterlein © &tradition.

Sticky Lamp
Photograph by Stefanie Grätz. Courtesy of Droog. Sticky Lamp, Chris Kabel © Droog.

Sticky Lamp
Photograph by Stefanie Grätz. Courtesy of Droog. Sticky Lamp, Chris Kabel © Droog.

Styrene
Photograph by Richard Brine: www.richardbrine.co.uk. Styrene, Paul Cocksedge © Paul Cocksedge.

Glo-Ball
Courtesy of Flos SpA. Glo-Ball, Jasper Morrison © Flos SpA.

Glo-Ball
Photograph by Ramak Fazel. Courtesy of Flos SpA. Glo-Ball, Jasper Morrison © Flos SpA.

Light Tray
Photograph Kalle Sanner and Daniel Rybakken. Light Tray, Andreas Engesvik and Daniel Rybakken, Asplund © Asplund.

28 series
Photograph by Gwenael Lewis. Courtesy of Bocci. 28 Series, Omer Arbel © Bocci.

Lighthouse
Photograph by Peter Guenzel. Courtesy of Established & Sons, London. Lighthouse, Ronan and Erwan Bouroullec © Established & Sons, London.

NeON
Photograph by Richard Brine: www.richardbrine.co.uk. NeON, Paul Cocksedge © Paul Cocksedge.

Diamonds are a girl's best friend
Courtesy of Meta. Diamonds Are a Girl's Best Friend, Matali Crasset, Meta © Meta

Copper Shade
Photograph by Tom Mannion. Courtesy of Tom Dixon. Copper Shade, Tom Dixon © Tom Dixon.

Fold
Photograph by Peter Guenzel. Courtesy of Established & Sons, London. Fold, Alexander Taylor © Established & Sons, London.

Beat
Photograph by Helene Bangsbo Andersen. Courtesy of Tom Dixon. Beat Light, Tom Dixon © Tom Dixon.

Heavy Light
Courtesy of Benjamin Hubert. Heavy Light, Benjamin Hubert © Benjamin Hubert.

Brave New World Lamp
Courtesy of Moooi. Brave New World Lamp, Freshwest © Moooi.

w084t2
Photograph by Philip Karlberg. Courtesy of Wästberg. w084t2, Studioilse © Wästberg

Wood Lamp
Photograph by Joakim Bergström. Courtesy of Muuto. Wood Lamp, TAF/Gabriella Gustafson & Mattias Ståhlbom © Muuto.

w101
Photograph by Philip Karlberg. Courtesy of Wästberg. w101, Claesson Koivisto Rune © Wästberg.

Pleated Lamp
Pleated Lamp, Inga Sempe © Cappellini.

Flex Lamp
Photograph by Gerard van Hees. Courtesy of Droog. Flex Lamp, Sam Hecht and Kim Colin/Industrial Facility © Droog.

Torch Light
Photograph by Peter Guenzel. Courtesy of Established & Sons, London. Torch Light, Sylvain Willenz © Established & Sons, London.

Hope
Photograph by Santi Caleca. Courtesy of Luceplan SpA. Hope, Francisco Gomez Paz and Paolo Rizzatto © Luceplan SpA.

Hope
Photograph by Tom Vack. Courtesy of Luceplan SpA. Hope, Francisco Gomez Paz and Paolo Rizzatto © Luceplan SpA.

Miss K
Photograph by Germano Borrelli. Courtesy of Flos SpA. Miss K, Philippe Starck © Flos SpA.

Miss K
Courtesy of Flos SpA. Miss K, Philippe Starck © Flos SpA.

Mite and Tite
Courtesy of Foscarini SRL. Mite and Tite, Marc Sadler © Foscarini SRL.

Hanabi
Photograph by Masayuki Hayashi. Courtesy of Nendo. Hanabi, Nendo © Nendo.

Technology

Random
Courtesy of Moooi. Random, Bertjan Pot © Moooi.

Random
Photograph by Inga Powilleit. Styling Tatjana Quax. Courtesy of Moooi. Random, Bertjan Pot © Moooi.

Tenda
Courtesy of Benjamin Hubert. Tenda, Benjamin Hubert © Benjamin Hubert.

Etch
Photograph by Tom Mannion. Courtesy of Tom Dixon. Etch, Tom Dixon © Tom Dixon.

Fragile Future
Courtesy of Carpenters Workshop Gallery. Fragile Future, Lonneke Gordijn and Ralph Nauta. © Carpenters Workshop Gallery/Mondrian Ltd.

Court Circuit
Courtesy of Danese. Court Circuit, Matali Crasset © Danese.

Hexalights
Courtesy of Marcus Tremonto. Hexalights, Marcus Tremonto © Marcus Tremonto.

Plumen 001
Photograph by Andrew Penketh. Courtesy of Hulger. Plumen 001, Hulger © Hulger.

Plumen 001
Photograph by Ian Nolan. Courtesy of Hulger. Plumen 001, Hulger © Hulger.

EL.E.Dee
Photograph © Tom Vack, Munich. Courtesy of Ingo Maurer GmbH. EL.E.Dee, Ingo Maurer © Ingo Maurer GmbH.

Kelvin LED
Courtesy of Flos SpA. Kelvin LED, Antonio Citterio with Toan Nguyen © Flos SpA.

CSYS
Courtesy of Jake Dyson. CSYS, Jake Dyson © Jake Dyson.

My New Flame
Photograph by Tom Vack, Munich. Courtesy of Ingo Maurer GmbH. My New Flame, Moritz Waldemeyer © Ingo Maurer GmbH.

Little Sun
Photograph by Merklit Mersha. Courtesy of Studio Olafur Eliasson. Little Sun, Olafur Eliasson and Frederik Ottesen © Little Sun GmbH.

Little Sun
Photograph by Omelga Mthiyane. Courtesy of Studio Olafur Eliasson. Little Sun, Olafur Eliasson and Frederik Ottesen © Little Sun GmbH.

Raimond
Courtesy of Moooi. Raimond, Raimond Puts © Moooi.

Thixotropes
Courtesy of Troika. Thixoptropes, Troika © Troika.

Wallpiercing
Courtesy of Flos SpA. Wallpiercing, Ron Gilad © Flos SpA.

SLAB
Courtesy of Carpenters Workshop Gallery. SLAB, Johanna Grawunder © Carpenters Workshop Gallery/Mondrian Ltd.

LED wallpaper
Photograph by Antoine Boote, New York. Courtesy of Ingo Maurer GmbH. LED Wallpaper, Ingo Maurer © Ingo Maurer GmbH.

LED wallpaper
Photograph by Raymond Vamin, New York. Courtesy of Ingo Maurer GmbH. LED Wallpaper, Ingo Maurer © Ingo Maurer GmbH.

Circles and Countercircles
Courtesy of Troika. Circles and Countercircles, Troika © Troika.

Family of OLEDs
Photograph by Johanna Schoemaker and Jonas Buck. Courtesy of Johanna Schoemaker. Family of OLEDs, Johanna Schoemaker © Johanna Schoemaker.

Flying Future
Photograph by Tom Vack, Munich. Courtesy of Ingo Maurer GmbH. Flying Future, Ingo Maurer © Ingo Maurer GmbH.

Edge
Photograph by Peter Guenzel. Courtesy of Established & Sons, London. Edge, Amanda Levete © Established & Sons, London.

Digital Dawn
Courtesy of Loop.pH. Digital Dawn, Rachel Wingfield © Rachel Wingfield.

Daylight Entrance
Photograph by Kalle Sanner and Daniel Rybakken. Daylight Entrance, © Daniel Rybakken.

Airborne Collection
Photograph © Christopher Moore. Courtesy of Catwalking. Airborne, Hussein Chalayan © Hussein Chalayan.

Airborne Collection
Photograph © Christopher Moore. Courtesy of Catwalking. Airborne, Hussein Chalayan © Hussein Chalayan.

SNOG Chelsea
Courtesy of Cinimod Studio. SNOG, Cinimod Studio © Cinimod Studio.

Awakening Lamp
Photograph by Anna Lonnerstam. Awakening Lamp, Front © Front.

Self Portrait
Courtesy of rAndom International. Self Portrait © rAndom International.

Lolita
Courtesy of Ron Arad Associates. Lolita, Ron Arad © Ron Arad Associates

You Fade to Light
Courtesy of Random International. You Fade to Light, rAndom International © rAndom International.

Bourrasque
Photograph by Mark Cocksedge. Bourrasque, Paul Cocksedge © Mark Cocksedge

Tree
Courtesy of Simon Heijdens. Tree, Simon Heijdens © Simon Heijdens.

Sonumbra
Courtesy of Loop.pH. Sonumbra, Rachel Wingfield and Mathias Gmachl © Loop.pH.

Volume
Photographed by John Adrian for UnitedVisualArtists. Volume, UVA © UVA.

Volume
Courtesy of UnitedVisualArtists. Volume, UVA © UVA.

OUTRACE
Photograph by David Levene. Courtesy of KRAM/WEISSHAAR AB. Outrace, KRAM/WEISSHAAR © Clemens Weisshaar and Reed Kram.

OUTRACE
Photograph by Mathias Ziegler. Courtesy of KRAM/WEISSHAAR AB. Outrace, KRAM/WEISSHAAR © Clemens Weisshaar and Reed Kram.

Solar Tree
Photograph by Ashley Bingham. Courtesy of Artemide GmbH. Solar Tree, Ross Lovegrove © Artemide GmbH.

Speed of Light
Photograph by Alan McAteer. NVA's Speed of Light, Edinburgh © NVA.

BIX
Photograph © 2003 by Angelo Kaunat. Courtesy of realities:united. BIX, realities:united © realities:united.

BIX
Photograph © 2003 by Harry Schiffer. Courtesy of realities:united. BIX, realities:united © realities:united.

Dream Cube Shanghai Corporate Pavilion
Photograph by Basil Childers. Courtesy of ESI Design. Dream Cube, ESI Design © ESI Design.

Showtime
Courtesy of Jason Bruges Studio. Showtime, Jason Bruges Studio © Jason Bruges Studio.